THE
BLUE BOOK
OF
FREEDOM

PRAISE FOR R. J. RUMMEL'S NONFICTION BOOKS

THE
BLUE BOOK OF FREEDOM

Ending Famine, Poverty, Democide, and War

R. J. RUMMEL

CUMBERLAND HOUSE
NASHVILLE, TENNESSEE

THE BLUE BOOK OF FREEDOM
PUBLISHED BY CUMBERLAND HOUSE PUBLISHING, INC.
431 Harding Industrial Drive
Nashville, Tennessee 37211

Cover design by Duncan Design, Nashville, Tennessee

Library of Congress Cataloging-in-Publication Data

Rummel, R. J. (Rudolph J.), 1932–
     The Blue book of freedom : ending famine, poverty, democide, and war /
     R.J. Rummel.
          p. cm.
     Includes bibliographical references.
     ISBN-13: 978-1-58182-620-3 (pbk. : alk. paper)
     ISBN-13: 978-1-68442-295-1(hc)
     1. Liberty. 2. Democracy. 3. Social justice. 4. Peace. I. Title.
JC585.R853 2007
320.01'1—dc22   2007023892

*For all those men and women who fight
and die so that others may be free.*

CONTENTS

THE
BLUE BOOK
OF
FREEDOM

1

OVERVIEW

MOST OF THE WORLD'S people have been robbed of their freedom by one dictatorship or another. Some, like the former regimes of Hitler, Stalin, Mao, Pol Pot, Kim Il-sung, and dozens of others, were more than just dictatorships. Their tyrannical dictators were slave masters ruling their people by their slightest whims and desires and those of their henchmen. These poor people lived in constant fear for themselves and their loved ones. And they were murdered by the hundreds of millions. In the last century alone 272,000,000 were shot, burned, stabbed, tortured, beaten, starved to death, blasted to death, buried alive, or whatever other ways of murdering their slaves these thugs could imagine. This horrific and evil toll of bodies could head-to-toe circle the earth more than ten times. It as though a catastrophic nuclear war had happened, but its mountain of deaths spread over each day of the last century.

The present existence of these ruling thugs in Burma, Cuba, Libya, North Korea, Saudi Arabia, Sudan, Syria, and

Turkmenistan, among others, creates an unbridgeable chasm in the world. On one side are such criminal gangs, sanctified by the term *government*, and the United Nations they dominate, enforcing by their guns mass slavery, mass death, mass violence, mass impoverishment, and mass famines. On the other side are democratic countries where people are free, secure, and need not fear mass impoverishment, murder at the hands of government agents, and killing famines.

This chasm between life and death, security and fear, on the same planet and at the same time, must no longer be tolerated. Dictatorships, even if benign, are by their very existence a crime against humanity and must be eliminated. However, the intellectuals, commentators, analysts, academics, and reporters of the democracies have identified power with greatness, thugs with statesmen, and propaganda with results. We have allowed moral and cultural relativism to silence our outrage, while conceding the moral high ground to the utopian dreamers; we have refused to recognize evil as evil; we have ignored the catastrophic human cost of such confusions and the natural and moral right to freedom.

What is so often ignored is that all people everywhere want to be democratically free, to exercise their human rights that are theirs by natural and international law and by an implicit social contract. Were this the only justification for freedom, it would be sufficient to make spreading freedom the ultimate policy.

But there is more to freedom than this. Much more. It provides the most important moral goods that humanity can desire. First:

The more people are free, the greater their human
development and national wealth. In short,
freedom is the way to economic and
social human security.

Still, human security involves more than wealth and prosperity. There is the security of knowing that one's life and the lives of loved ones are safe from deadly famines. Therefore, second:

Free people never have famines.

But as important as these moral goods are, they do not deal with the worst hell to which billions of human beings are still subject: torture, rape, beatings, forced labor, genocide, mass murder, executions, deportations, political violence, and war. With no human rights, billions live in fear for their lives and for those of their loved ones. There is a third moral good of freedom:

Where people are free,
political violence is minimal.

Where people are not free—as in Burma, Sudan, and North Korea—they are only pieces on a playing board for the armed thugs and gangs that oppress them, rape them, loot them, exploit them, and murder them.

The gangs that control these so-called governments oppress whole nations under cover of international law. They are like a gang that captures a group of hikers and then does with them what they will: robbing all, torturing and murdering some because gang members don't like them or they are "disobedient," and raping others.

And they murder their slaves by whim, by hatred, by quota, and sometimes for no reason at all. The worst of these gangs are megamurderers with their victims reaching into the tens of millions. Such murder is democide, and its elimination as one of humanity's plagues is the greatest of all moral goods.

The fourth moral good of freedom is this:

> The more freedom a people have, the more unlikely the government will murder them. Democratically free governments do not murder their own people.

This huge moral split in the world between governing thugs who murder their slaves wholesale and free people who fear no such personal disaster for them or their loved ones is unconscionable and unacceptable. It is time for concerted nonviolent action to eliminate these criminal thugs and free their slaves.

However, there is still one more moral good that even more strengthens this moral imperative:

> The less free the people within any two nations are, the bloodier and more destructive the wars between them; the greater their freedom, the less likely such wars occur. Free people do not make war on each other.

What this means is that we do not have to wait for all, or almost all, nations to become democracies in order to reduce the severity of war. As we promote freedom, as the people of more and more nations gain greater human rights and political liberties, as those people without any freedom become partly free, we will decrease the bloodiness of the world's wars. In short:

> Increasing freedom in the world decreases the death toll of its wars. Surely, whatever reduces and then finally ends the scourge of war in our history, without causing a greater evil, must be the greatest moral good. And this is freedom.

The implications of all these moral goods of freedom for foreign policy and international activism are profound:

> to promote global human security, to do away with famine, mass impoverishment, democide, and war, and to minimize internal violence, promote freedom.

Since peace, national security, and national and global welfare are the paramount concerns of a democratic nation's foreign policy, its overriding goal should be to peacefully promote human rights and democratic freedom. This should be the bottom line of international negotiations, treaties, foreign aid, and military action (if necessary for defense or humanitarian reasons—as in Kosovo, Bosnia, Afghanistan, or Iraq). As to defense policy, military planning usually is based on assessments of the intentions and capability of others. What is clear is that the less free the people of a nation are, the more we should beware of the intentions of their rulers. In other words, it is not the democracies of the world that we need to defend against.

Moreover, consider what the peace-creating power of freedom means for nuclear weapons. Many people are justly worried about the ultimate danger to humanity—nuclear war. They protest and demonstrate against nuclear weapons. Some cross the line and engage in illegal activities, such as destroying military property, and risk prison to draw public attention to the cataclysmic danger of such weapons. Were these dedicated people to spend even half this effort on promoting freedom and human rights for the people of the most powerful dictatorships that have or may soon have such weapons—for instance, China, North Korea, and Iran—they would be striking at the root cause of the risk of nuclear war.

The power of freedom to end war, minimize violence within nations, and eradicate genocide and mass murder almost seems magical. It is as though we have a single-drug cure for cancer, but in the case of freedom, it is all true and well established.

Our knowledge of the peace-creating and peacemaking effects of freedom now gives us a nonviolent way to promote a nonviolent world. The ultimate conclusions of this book are:

Power kills, and absolute power kills absolutely.

and

Democratic freedom is a method of nonviolence.

2

THE RIGHTS OF ALL PEOPLE

PEOPLE THE WORLD OVER—whether Christian, Muslim, or Buddhist; European, African, Asian, or Indian; North or South; rich or poor—want to be free, with all the human rights that are justly theirs by international and natural law. Broadly speaking, a person's rights, whatever they may be, define the scope of individual freedom. In the Western tradition of freedom, these are their civil and political rights, including freedom of speech, religion, and association.

Some philosophers see these not only as morally justified rights in themselves but also as the means for fulfilling other possible rights, like happiness. The opposing position is that such rights have no special status unless granted by a government:

to maintain tradition, as does an absolute monarchy like Saudi Arabia
to pursue a just society, as the Communist Party of China claims

to protect a holy society, as does a Muslim government
like that in Sudan

to economically develop a country, as attempted by a
military government like that in Burma.

The internationally popular justification for a people's
freedom is by reference to human rights, namely, those due
to individuals as human beings. The term human rights is
recent in origin. President Franklin Delano Roosevelt first
used it in a 1941 message to the U.S. Congress, when he
declared that everyone has four human rights—freedom of
speech and religion and freedom from want and fear.

Since 1941, there has been a vigorous international affir-
mation of these and other human rights. Many a nation's
constitution has included them, and they now are part of an
international bill of rights. The latter comprises Articles 1
and 55 of the 1945 U.N. Charter, the 1948 Universal Declaration of Human Rights adopted by the U.N. General Assembly, and the two international covenants passed by the
General Assembly in 1966, one on civil and political rights,
and the other on economic, social, and cultural rights.

The most basic of all these rights are those defining what
governments cannot do to their own people. From those
stated in the Universal Declaration of Human Rights, these
include everyone's right:

- to life, liberty, and personal security
- to recognition as a person before the law, equal protection of the law, remedy for violation of their rights, fair
  and public trial, and the presumption of innocence
  until proven guilty if charged with a penal offense

- to leave any country and return and to seek asylum from persecution
- to secret ballots, periodic elections, and freely chosen representatives
- to form and join trade unions
- to equal access to public service and participation in cultural life
- to freedom of movement and residence, thought, conscience and religion, opinion, and expression
- to peaceful assembly and association
- to choose, as parents, their children's education
- to freedom from slavery or servitude, torture, degrading or inhuman treatment or punishment, arbitrary arrest or detention or exile
- to freedom from arbitrary interference with privacy or family or home or correspondence
- to freedom from deprivation of nationality, arbitrary deprivation of property, or being compelled to join an association

These human rights define democratic freedom. A people's freedom of thought, expression, religion, and association are basic, as are secret ballots, periodic elections, and the right to representation. In short, these rights say that people have a right to be free. Condemning the lack of freedom in the worst of the thugdoms, North Korea for example, is not imposing our values on another culture. This is not a matter of value relativity. Demanding human rights, and thus freedom, for the slaves in the Sudan—or for Chinese political prisoners, or for women in Muslim countries, or for Burmese forced laborers—is simply demanding that their ruling gangs obey international law, which is itself based on general treaties, international agreements, and practices.

This law is universal. Every Arabian, Chinese, Rwandan, and all the world's peoples have the internationally defined and protected human rights listed above. As the bodies of murdered men, women, and children accumulate by the hundreds of millions, it is way past time to enforce international law.

3

THE JUSTNESS OF FREEDOM

HUMAN RIGHTS IN A democracy are a social contract that people would enter into if blinded as to how the contract would benefit their race, social status, or occupation personally. Aside from natural and international law, this is the philosophical justification for democracy. At its heart, there are two democratic axioms.

> **Free Choice:** People have a right to form their own community or group.

> **Free Exit:** People have a right to leave any community or group.

Together, these freedoms give everyone the right to organize with each other a community governed by their own principles and with whatever rights they want, as long as they do not force this community on others and anyone is free to leave it.

In short, people would be free to be unfree, if that is the kind of community they wish to join, and this is part of what democratic freedom means. The human or natural right to be free implies the right of free choice. Free speech does not mean that one has to speak out; one can say nothing if one wishes, or one can join a group in which this freedom is strictly circumscribed or even totalitarian in governance, such as the military or a monastery. Freedom of religion means that if people so desire, they can form a group in which only one religion is legitimate and they may exclude those of other religions, as in a Catholic nunnery. And within liberal democracies today, people usually can support and participate in antidemocratic political parties and movements. The Communist Party, for example, is legal in the United States and most other democracies.

As a result of these two democratic axioms,

> Democracy is a metasolution to
> the problem of diversity.

Democracy unites, under one government, people who are vastly different socially, culturally, and philosophically. Democracy says, "Govern yourself, but do so in a manner consistent with the same right of others." Democracy does not lay down a template for each person's life, as do dictatorships. Rather, as a metasolution to the principles for the greater society, it is a method of governance that prevents possible bloody conflicts over rights, means, and ends.

Throughout eons of human history, through the growth and collapse of clans and cities, nations and states, civilizations and empires; through the many human disasters and catastrophes, wars and revolutions; through the growth and decay of religions and creeds, philosophies, and ideologies; and through the countless day-by-day interactions of billions of people, a system of world governance has evolved based, in effect, on these two democratic axioms.

The most basic right people have in the modern international system is that of self-determination for their country or national group, with its allied international legal principle of state sovereignty. This, unfortunately, has meant that gangs of thugs can seize power over a country, and once they have it, they become a legal government, sovereign and independent. This is the contradiction in international law. For while being sovereign, these gangs use it to horribly violate their people's human rights.

Nonetheless, the idea of self-determination has had tremendous power in international relations. It was the force behind demands for independence by the former British, French, Dutch, Portuguese, and Spanish colonies. Against the cries for self-determination, these nations could no longer justify their undemocratic and remote imperial rule. Within a few decades after World War II, much of the world was decolonized, and by the end of the Soviet Empire in 1991, no more than a few small and scattered colonies remained.

A corollary to the principle of sovereignty is that no other nation has a right to intervene in a nation's domestic affairs. The principle, really a metaprinciple, of sovereignty legally allows a community to govern itself with great freedom. Although by their agreements and treaties nations have placed certain restrictions on this sovereignty—such as restricting the right to carry out genocide or slavery, and obligating all governments to respect certain human rights—each nation still is nearly free to govern itself.

And although this is not respected by all countries, international law gives everyone the right to immigrate and, particularly, to request political asylum of another nation. This is, in effect, the principle of free exit.

So, through many millenniums of civilizations, empires, city-states, nations, alliances, wars, and revolutions, the world's peoples have slowly evolved a metasolution to their vastly different societies and cultures, just as a species evolves in response to its environment. This real-world metasolution has globally institutionalized the rights of free choice and free exit.

4

THE INSTITUTIONS OF DEMOCRACY

A DEMOCRACY NECESSARILY INVOLVES an electoral system through which people choose their representatives and leaders. They thus give their consent to be governed by those who reflect their interests. The manner in which democracies conduct their elections varies, but all share these characteristics: regular elections for high office, secret ballots, a franchise that includes nearly the whole adult population, and competitive elections.

Real competition in elections is a key requirement. Many Communist nations exhibited all the electoral characteristics mentioned in their periodic election of legislators handpicked by the Communist Party, who then simply rubberstamped what the party wanted. "Competitive" means that those running for office reflect different political beliefs and positions on the issues. If they do not, as in the Communist nations, then the government is not democratic.

Besides its electoral characteristics, one kind of democracy has characteristics crucial for freedom. These involve the recognition of certain human rights discussed previously. One is the freedom to organize political groups or parties, even if they represent a small radical minority, that then may nominate their members to run for high office. Another right entitles people to an open, transparent government—in particular, the right to know how one's representatives voted and debated. There are also the right to freedom of speech (particularly as exercised by newspapers and other media to criticize government policies and leaders), the right to freedom of religion, and the right to form unions and organize businesses.

One of the most important of these rights is the right to a fair trial as provided under the rule of law. Above the state, there must be a law that structures the government and elaborates the reciprocal rights and duties of the government and the people, which all governing officials and their policies must obey. This is a constitution, either created as a single document, like that of the United States, or a set of documents, statutes, and traditions, such as that of Great Britain.

If a democracy recognizes these rights, it is called a liberal democracy. If it does not—if it has electoral characteristics but suppresses freedom of speech, possesses leaders who put themselves above the law, and representatives who make and vote on policies in secret—then it is called a procedural or an electoral democracy.

For the term *liberal democracy,* the root definition of "liberal" is meant, not its modern political meaning. A liberal democracy means that a people rule themselves through periodic elections in which nearly all adults can participate. They elect their highest leaders to the offices for which they are eligible, and they are governed under the rule of law that guarantees them certain human rights.

Of the 192 nations in the world in 2006, 121 were democracies, and 89 of these were liberal—free—democracies, which is a sharp increase from the 44 that existed in 1973. For a world population of about 6.3 billion, 2.8 billion live in liberal democracies, while 2.2 billion live in partly free or in unfree countries ruled by thugs who enslave them.

CLINTON'S IMPEACHMENT

Consider an example that illustrates the nature of liberal democracy in action: the 1998/99 impeachment and trial of U.S. President William Jefferson Clinton. The impeachment was a deeply divisive, partisan political battle, and most Americans developed strong opinions supporting and opposing it. After all, this was a matter of determining whether the nationally elected president of the United States would be fired.

In his first term in office, Clinton's opponents forced him to respond to allegations of wrongdoing committed while he was governor of Arkansas, involving investments that he and his wife, Hillary Rodham Clinton, had made in the Whitewater Development Corporation, an Arkansas real estate development firm. Revelations and questions about this, and associated affairs having to do with the savings and loans firm Madison Guaranty, eventually led to a federal investigation by an independent counsel. The House and Senate banking committees also held hearings on the Whitewater affair.

Notice that democratic leaders cannot escape the law, even regarding what they might have done before being elected or appointed to office. Prosecutors may investigate their past and present activities, force them to testify before a grand jury, indict them, and even bring them to trial. This contributes to what keeps democracies limited, which is their checks and balances system. This means that the executive, legislature, and judiciary are in constant competition against each other for power and influence, and they watch each other for opportunities to gain an advantage or weaken one another.

However, the one scandal that finally led to the president's impeachment involved Paula Jones, a former clerk in the Arkansas state government. Jones alleged that, while Clinton was governor of Arkansas in 1991, a state trooper invited her to the governor's hotel room, and when she was alone in the room with the governor, he dropped his pants and asked her for oral sex. The White House and the president's supporters responded aggressively to these charges and tried to undermine Jones's credibility through personal attacks.

Angered by these attacks, Jones filed a civil suit of sexual harassment against President Clinton and demanded $700,000 and a personal apology. Working through his lawyers, Clinton appealed the suit and asked for a delay until after his term was over. But the Supreme Court ruled that the suit should go ahead. After more legal twists, turns, and appeals, including Jones's upping her demand to a million dollars, Clinton settled the case in 1999 by sending her a check for $850,000 but offering no apology.

No matter how powerful a democratic president is, no matter how much support he has, any citizen can sue him in court. Just as important, despite the president's power, the

White House sources at his disposal, his small army of lawyers, his broad support in the media, and his popularity, the judiciary can force the president to defend himself in court according to the law, even though, in military terms, Clinton was the most powerful head of any country in the world. Moreover, he, his lawyers, and his supporters used the major media (which supported him), every technical legal device ever written into law, and any possible wayward interpretation of the law to claim that Jones had no right to sue him. The absolutely critical point here is that it all was to no avail. In a liberal democracy, the law rules. In this case, no matter what twists and turns were employed by the president, the law sided with a little-known clerk from Arkansas.

While this suit was under way, Clinton began an eighteen-month affair in the White House and the Oval Office with twenty-two-year-old Monica Lewinsky, a White House intern. Although President Clinton disputes that he had sexual relations with Lewinsky, she did give him oral sex, a fact later proved by a DNA test of the semen on a dress she wore during one of these meetings. There is nothing in the law against sexual affairs in the White House, but the president might have broken several laws on other matters, including possible sexual harassment of Lewinsky, asking her to lie in court, and bribing her to keep quiet.

By decision of the Supreme Court, Clinton had to give a pretrial, videotaped deposition in the Jones suit. In January 1998, with Jones sitting across from him, Jones's lawyers questioned Clinton for six hours. He had no idea that they knew about his affair with Lewinsky, and he was quite surprised when they brought it up. Given a broad definition of sexual relations, approved by the judge sitting in on the deposition, Clinton denied under oath that he had sexual relations—as defined by the judge at the deposition—with Lewinsky, and he claimed that he did not remember ever being alone with her in the White House.

Clinton also had to answer questions before a grand jury, done with a closed-circuit television hookup to the White House. He answered many questions about the Lewinsky affair and information she had provided, but he would not answer any questions about their sexual relation.

In September 1998, independent counsel Kenneth W. Starr submitted a report on this scandal to the House of Representatives, as required by law. It was, in effect, a 453-page indictment of the president, listing eleven allegedly impeachable offenses. The House almost immediately released the full report to the public, as well as thousands of pages of evidence soon thereafter. Within days, the House Judiciary Committee also made public the full videotape of the president's testimony before the grand jury.

This openness well illustrates the transparency of a liberal democracy. Opponents or proponents will disclose all that is politically important, including dirty laundry, about some politician, legislation, or policy. This is a crucial role of the opposition, and it is the reason why having a strong opposition is a basic ingredient of liberal democracy. They want to embarrass and weaken the party in power so they can turn into law their favored legislation and win the next election. Even supposedly secret testimony, conversations, and reports are exposed this way—as is a mass of trivia. Surely, partisans on all sides will spin whatever is disclosed to show its best or worst side. But all of this is public, and people are free to make of it what they will.

When the Republican-controlled Judiciary Committee began consideration of a resolution calling for a formal impeachment inquiry, the fight was now formally joined and in deadly earnest, yet still constrained by the Constitution and House rules. This began the long, complex political process for removing Clinton from office.

Other than wartime, the legal process of removing a democratically elected chief executive in midterm is the most dramatic theater experienced by people in democracies. Everyone soon knows almost everything public and private about the cast of characters; the acting is superb, the speeches and exhortations moving, and the appeals to mind and heart well studied. Each day is a new scene, the plot is clear, and only the end is in doubt.

A successful impeachment by the House is like an indictment brought by a prosecutor before a court. It describes the particulars of an alleged wrongdoing. Then, before a judge, a court holds the trial on the indictment, with both prosecutors and defense lawyers presenting evidence and arguments. The Constitution specifies "treason, bribery, or other high crimes and misdemeanors" as the grounds for impeachment, but what "high crimes and misdemeanors" are is subject to considerable legal interpretation. Only a majority vote of the House is enough to approve articles of impeachment, and this had only happened once before, in 1868 against President Andrew Johnson.

Once the House votes on impeachment, the Senate holds a trial on the impeachment articles. All senators sit as the jury, and the chief justice of the Supreme Court presides over the trial. The senators hear witnesses and can interrogate them, and at the end of the trial, they vote regarding removal of the president. Two-thirds of the senators must approve removal for it to occur. Were this to happen, the chief justice would swear in the vice president as the new president. The Senate vote on Johnson's removal was one vote short of two-thirds.

The House Judiciary Committee reported to the full House on its recommendation to investigate the impeachment of President Clinton, and in October 1998, the Republican House voted to conduct this investigation. Hearings by the House Judiciary Committee on impeachment began soon afterward and were fully televised.

At the end of the hearings, the Republican members presented the committee with four articles of impeachment, claiming that the president committed perjury before the grand jury, obstruction of justice in the Jones case, and provided false responses to eighty-one questions. The committee approved the articles on December 11 and 12. All Republicans voted for three of the articles, and all but one voted for a fourth; no Democrat voted for any.

The committee then passed the approved articles to the full House for debate and a final vote. After an acrimonious debate on the impeachment of President Clinton, the House passed 228-to-206 the first article of impeachment, perjury before Independent Starr's grand jury. It also passed the third article, obstruction of justice related to the Jones case, with a vote of 221 to 212. The other two articles failed to pass. It was up to the Senate to determine whether these two articles were enough to remove the president from office.

The Senate trial began on January 7, 1999, and was televised throughout. As dictated by the Constitution, the chief justice of the Supreme Court, William H. Rehnquist, presided over the trial. The trial started with a reading of the charges, and then the chief justice swore in the senators, who went one at a time to the front of the chamber to sign an oath book promising "impartial justice." There were fifty-five Republican and forty-five Democratic senators. If all Republicans voted for removal, twelve Democrats would have to join them to get the sixty-seven votes required.

Both sides presented their arguments and evidence in three days, and the senators had two more days to ask questions. As the trial progressed, Democrats and Republicans used one partisan maneuver after another, although with less bitterness than in the House debate. Finally, on February 8, this twelve-month, historic crisis in American politics neared its conclusion. Each side had three hours in which to present their closing arguments, then for three days the senators debated behind closed doors. On February 12, in the Senate chamber and before television cameras, the Senate voted. All Democrats and ten Republicans voted President Clinton not guilty on alleged perjury, 55 to 45. On alleged obstruction of justice, the vote was split, 50 to 50. Clinton would remain in office.

Generally, answers to specific questions in the polls showed that arguments supporting President Clinton persuaded more people than arguments demanding his removal. The senators were, after all, politicians, and doubtless were influenced in their votes by public opinion. Indeed, because of the overwhelming public support for Clinton, the Republican Senate leadership had decided against trying to fire Clinton and had organized the trial to get it over with as soon as possible.

What do the campaigns, scandals, and the impeachment of President Clinton tell us about the nature and workings of a liberal democracy? It is self-government. Throughout the history of the Clinton presidency, adult Americans could have campaigned and voted for Clinton or his opposition in the presidential elections of 1992 and 1996. Americans could also have campaigned and voted for the representatives and senators who voted on his impeachment and removal. Americans could make their voices heard regarding his scandals and impeachment by writing letters to the editors of newspapers, telephoning radio talk shows, or by posting their opinions for or against him on the Internet via chat groups or on their own Web page. And Americans could organize demonstrations or participate in them, build organizations to work for or against him, and contribute money to one side or the other.

There also is a democratic culture involved. This dictates that compromise and negotiation will settle disputes with a tolerance for differences. If the conflict is profound and the stakes very high, if there is no solution other than one side losing and the other side winning, then democratic procedures must be used that are within or dictated by the law. Such was the impeachment and trial of President Clinton.

But consider: the president had vast public and secret resources at his disposal, such as the Secret Service, the FBI, and the CIA. As commander in chief, he had all U.S. military forces at his command. Could he not have used this power, if he so desired, to have the army surround Congress and the Supreme Court and dictate the outcome of their impeachment proceedings? That this was not even considered by anyone in the media, that there was not the slightest rumor of this, that even his most extreme political enemies never thought this a possibility, shows the strength of this liberal democracy.

THE PRESIDENTIAL ELECTION OF 2000

One more example of the nature of liberal democracy is the outcome of the 2000 American presidential election. The Democratic candidate, Vice President Albert Gore, received a majority of the national vote and came within a couple hundred votes of winning Florida's electors, which would have given him the 270 electoral votes needed to become president. As it was, with Florida's slim margin giving the Republican candidate, Texas Governor George Bush, its electoral votes, Bush won the presidency with only 271 electoral votes.

Because of the importance of the Florida electors and the very slight margin of victory for Bush, Gore refused to concede the election, and he, his supporters, and the Democratic Party waged a public relations and legal on-slaught on the ballots cast in Florida, particularly in highly Democrat counties. They argued that all the ballots had not been counted, that the voting machines had malfunctioned, or that the ballots were too complex for many voters.

I need not go into the legal and political victories and defeats in this campaign to overturn Bush's victory. After two Florida Supreme Court victories for Gore and two U.S. Supreme Court decisions vacating or overturning them, Gore lost hope of getting the recount of the ballots that he wanted. More than a month after the election, Gore finally and graciously conceded the election to Bush.

This was the closest election in American history. And yet—and this is the point to this example—in spite of the heated partisan rhetoric and the claims that the election had been stolen, there was no violence. There were no violent demonstrations, no riots, no necessity to call out the army or National Guard, no coup attempt. The decision of the Supreme Court was accepted; law triumphed over the desire for power and over outrage at the result. This is almost unbelievable, considering that this election was to determine who would be the most powerful leader in the world and which economic and social policies would dominate the country. But it is the way liberal democracy functions.

Overall, the case for democratic freedom is strong. But I can make an even stronger case. In the following chapters, we'll see that freedom is not only a human or natural right, certified by international agreements and supported by moral reasoning. It is not only a socially just metasolution to human diversity, it is also a moral good. This means that the social and political consequences of freedom make it a supreme value in itself.

5

FREEDOM'S MORAL GOODS: WEALTH AND PROSPERITY

SOME RULING GANGS AND their supporters deny their people freedom by arguing that doing so is necessary to develop their country economically, achieve national glory, to promote racial or ethnic purity, to obey the laws of God or Mohammed, or to create a Communist paradise. This is to make of freedom a tool that those in power can manipulate or ignore, depending on the ends they seek. This is a destructive premise that, for too long, intellectuals have allowed dictators to assume.

Freedom is not a tool; it does not have a utility attached to it that justifies government's granting it or taking it away. In this sense, democratic freedom is a moral good, something that is to be sought or held for its intrinsic moral value and for no other reason. Yet, amazingly, there are actually consequences to freedom that are also important moral goods. When we compare what happens to an economy and a society when people are free and democratic versus unfree, the results of freedom are often the very ends that some dictators try to fulfill by repressing freedom. So stressing that freedom is a moral good is not erecting a firewall against any negative consequences, for the consequences are not only positive, but moral goods in themselves. It's like eating fruit, which is tasty and filling and inherently good, but which if eaten regularly also reduces the probability of getting cancer or suffering a stroke or heart attack.

For the world as a whole, there is a very strong, positive correlation between democratic freedom and the economic wealth and prosperity of nations. The richest and most productive countries in the world are liberal democracies. Much of this is due to the close association between democratic and economic freedom. And this positive correlation goes far beyond economic matters to include the social and physical welfare of a people as well.

The more freedom people have, the greater their nation's technological growth and scientific contributions and infrastructure (availability of railroads, paved roads, and airports). The more freedom people have, the better their health services, and the more and better their hospitals and doctors, and the longer their life expectancy. The more freedom a people have, the greater their literacy, the higher their proportion of high school and college graduates, the more numerous their universities and books published, and so on. To adopt a current term for all this, the more freedom, the more human security.

BILL GATES AND MICROSOFT

One of freedom's desirable consequences is to promote unrivaled wealth and prosperity; it is an unbeatable engine of technological and economic growth. As an example of how freedom can produce this miraculous result, consider the life of William "Bill" Gates, who could not have created Microsoft and the computer software he did other than in a free society—software that has contributed greatly to our prosperity.

In 1986, Microsoft successfully went public with its stock offering of $21 a share, and by 1995, Microsoft had 17,801 employees. Through his company, Gates has played a dominant role in making personal computing available to everyone, and his products have continued to dominate the field. I do my work on a Macintosh computer with an operating system that competes with Microsoft's operating system. While I believe Apple's system software is better, I use Microsoft's Word and Excel programs because of their quality.

In recognition of Gates's contributions, President George H. W. Bush awarded him the National Medal of Technology in 1992. Gates also has been more than amply rewarded financially. On May 22, 2000, his wealth, tied partly to the near 141 million shares of Microsoft that he owns, was $72,485,700,000. This made him the richest man in the world.

How can one man become so rich? Surely, Gates was lucky in being in the right place with the right friends at the right time when the personal computer revolution was just beginning. Supportive and affluent parents played a role in his success, as did his naturally deep interest in computers, a proclivity for the mathematics of it, and a willingness to work hard.

But most important, Gates was free to follow his star. He needed no government approval. Personal computers and related hardware and software were a new market, and there were virtually no government regulations telling Gates what programming he could and could not do. Of course, Gates and his partner at the time, Paul Allen, had to satisfy certain government registration requirements when they set up Microsoft, and there were more regulations covering Microsoft when it went public in the stock market. But it was entirely up to Gates as to how hard he worked, what he produced, and what he charged for his products.

Why should freedom be so productive? One reason is that people like Bill Gates can follow their interests and fully realize their inherent capabilities and talents. Also, they have an incentive to work and produce what people want because they are rewarded—and handsomely so, if they can satisfy the desires of millions. There is something more here, however, than simply following personal interests and getting material rewards. People naturally take care of what they own. It is like driving a rented automobile versus one's own car—in subtle and perhaps even in some extreme ways, one is probably rougher on the rental. After all, we lose nothing when we rapidly start and stop a rented car, corner it at high speed, screech its tires, grind its gears, ignore potholes, and let it get filthy. The rental cost is the same either way.

This is like the common areas of a neighborhood. People take care of their homes and yards. It is personal property and a reflection of their inner self, a matter of personal pride. But the commons, such as a public park, are owned by the public and therefore by no one. Government bureaucrats are the stewards over such property, and by law, they must manage it. But this is not their personal property, and therefore they do not have a primary motivation to take care of it and improve it. Usually, their personal motivation is to do the least amount of work at the best wage, and even if they do the best job possible, they do not do more than needed. So I see trees and flowers planted along newly built public roads soon withering and dying for lack of water, and I walk in parks whose grassy areas are overgrown with weeds and littered with the debris of people who use facilities they do not own. (I dare not think about using a public restroom!)

Besides the joys of freedom, the prosperity it creates, and the incentives of private ownership, there is individualization of choice and behavior. While people share much with their neighbors, friends, and loved ones, each person is different. Each person has values, perceptions, and experiences that no economic and social planners can know, or usually even guess at; in no way can each become data in some planner's computer, because the path through life for each is unique. This means that only individuals can best judge what they value, desire, want, and can do. To borrow a useful cliché, each alone knows where their shoe pinches.

This is more basic than it may at first seem. In the free market, everyone is free to buy and sell, to create and build—as did Bill Gates. This freedom enables everyone to best adjust to the world around them and apply their unique values and experience. Therefore, a farmer who has learned from his parents and by his own direct experience how to till the soil unique to northeastern Ohio, to read the local weather patterns, and to plant and fertilize the seeds that will grow well in the rocky soil will best know how to make his farm productive. No government official far away at the state capital in Columbus or the national capital in Washington, D.C., can do as well. And really, were they to command him how to farm, they would destroy both his incentive to produce and the farm's productivity. The loss of this freedom to farm is a loss of personal experience, personal knowledge, and personal values that government commands cannot replace.

Moreover, in a free market, buyers and sellers automatically balance the cost and amount of goods. This means it is often more profitable to sell many items at a small profit than a few at a high profit. This encourages lower prices and cheaper goods to meet the mass demand of poorer people. Some producers will specialize in building yachts and make a profit at it, but many others will find it more profitable to market less-expensive clothes, fast food, games, and thousands of devices that make life easier. And in this way, businesses are encouraged to produce more items, more cost effective, and of better quality. We have seen this regarding computers.

Note also, as free market economists like Milton Friedman, Ludwig von Mises, and F. A. Hayek have stressed, free market prices are an economy-wide message system. They communicate shortages, where things are cheap, and where production might be profitable enough for a business to move into the market. They also communicate where demand is slack and when businesses might cut back production. Prices in a free market tell businesses what to put on the supermarket shelves where, when, and at what price. Therefore, the free market is equally a massive distribution system.

Think about this for the moment, about the miracle of the thousands of goods on the supermarket shelves, many from faraway countries and other states. Who decides this? What great mind or computer figures out what is to be sold in what market for how much and when. And this is accomplished without shortages and without long lines waiting for a supply truck to arrive, which is often the case in command economies. How is this done without the economic planners that socialists believe necessary? It occurs automatically and spontaneously through the decisions of hundreds of thousands of free producers, suppliers, truckers, and market managers, all of whom respond to different prices and demand.

This is why the command market and government intervention fail to improve prices and allocation over the free market. Instead, it creates economic dislocations, hardships, privations, and, as we will see, famine. No government officials, no social scientists, no central computer program can possibly figure out what each person wants, when, and where and how all this can be balanced for tens of millions of people. A government cannot improve the free-market price mechanism, even at the minimum by antitrust, antimonopolistic laws. It can only distort or destroy it.

LENIN'S COMMAND ECONOMY

One may believe that I am exaggerating the role of freedom, that for Bill Gates's success, his talent and initiative were most important. Then consider what his life would have been like in a country that allowed no freedom, such as the former Soviet Union.

The Communist Party that ruled this country placed the strongest emphasis on economic and technological development, and it is natural to believe that someone with Gates's abilities and interests would prosper there. First, however, for Gates simply to survive without going to a labor camp or to his death, he and his parents could not question the party line, and both his parents and grandparents could not have been connected to the previous czarist government or be bourgeoisie. Presuming, then, that Gates was clean of any such "counterrevolutionary" taint, he might have succeeded as a scientist or engineer. But he could not have produced any great leap in software development.

The party strictly limited the use of computers, all of which it owned. For more than a decade, it kept computers under lock and key, to be used only with party permission. Gates, therefore, would not have had the free use of computers that enabled him to develop his programming ability and to eventually write the programs he did. And since all private businesses were illegal, there could be no Microsoft to design operating systems or create software. Such could only be done within party-run shops. If, in such a shop, Gates had written useful software, it would be the property of the party, to dispose of as the party bureaucracy wished.

In the twentieth century, the major competing model to the free market was that based on the economic and historical analysis presented in *Das Kapital,* written by the nineteenth-century German political philosopher Karl Marx. Along with Friedrich Engels, Marx established the "scientific" socialism that we now call communism. In his many works, including his influential pamphlet *What Is to Be Done,* Russian revolutionary and philosopher Vladimir Ilich Lenin showed how Marx and Engels's politico-economic theory could be put into effect—how a communist revolution could be induced and a communist nirvana achieved through the dictatorship of the proletariat. Scholars now believe his work is such a basic addition to Marxism that they make Marxism-Leninism synonymous with Communism.

Communism was the most influential politico-economic theory of the twentieth century. With its claims of empirical proof, a scientific theory of history, and its utopian plan to rid the world of poverty, exploitation, economic greed, and war (all of which it claims were due to capitalism), it captured the minds of many intellectuals and workers. And through revolution, invasion, and war, these believers took over one country after another: Russia, China, Mongolia, North Korea, Vietnam, Cambodia, Laos, Cuba, East Germany, Poland, Hungary, Rumania, Bulgaria, Yugoslavia, Czechoslovakia, Ethiopia, Angola, Mozambique, Grenada, Nicaragua, and South Yemen. This is an impressive roster indeed.

The Communist politico-economic model explicitly claims that while the free market will lead to the impoverishment of the worker and its own destruction, communism will create socioeconomic equality and a society in which abundance will reign and provide "from each according to their ability, and to each according to their need." This abstract model seems ideal and has misled many a compassionate person. But let us look at what this model really meant in practice for the former Soviet Union under Lenin and Stalin—compared to a free market.

First, what did Lenin achieve with his introduction of communism after the Red Army won control over much of Russia? The Communist Party—in effect, the new government of the Soviet Union—issued a Decree on Land that encouraged peasants to seize large estates, thus depriving cities and towns of food. This created much local disorder, as did the party's establishing committees of peasants to "assume the responsibility for repression" and the decree that officials in all small, grain-producing districts should pick twenty-five to thirty "wealthy" hostages to be killed if the peasants did not deliver their "excess" grain. In practice, excess grain often turned out to be any grain—even the peasants' reserve and seed grain was expropriated by detachments of workers ignorant of farming. The party sent tens of thousands of people from the cities to uncover the peasants' "excess," which resulted in more disarray that was hardly conducive to good harvests. As Lenin himself confessed, "Practically, we took all the surplus grain—and sometimes even not only surplus grain, but part of the grain the peasant required for food."

By 1920, in what was sometimes called War Communism, 30 percent of what peasants produced was requisitioned. It was no longer necessary that Lenin requisition supplies for the Red Army's conflict with the anti-Communist White armies, since they were defeated. Rather, Lenin's purpose was to move from a capitalist free market to a socialist one—to a command economy, as he declared. He wanted to nationalize the peasants, although not in the total way that Stalin would do a decade later through collectivization.

Nationalization and its attendant forced requisitions was Lenin's solution to the problem of paying for the peasants' grain when funds were not available. And it prevented peasants from keeping their grain and other crops from the party. The party also made many new laws to assure this. It set low prices for the peasants' produce, banned private trade, and established a system of rationing. Unlike a free market, this provided little motivation to produce—notwithstanding the likelihood of new detachments of workers coming through to expropriate or loot whatever was in a field, barn, or house. Understandably, the harvest of 1921 was only 40 percent that of 1913, before the revolution.

This disastrous harvest, coupled with the loss (or consumption due to hunger) of the reserve food supplies necessary for the peasants to survive periodic droughts, had human costs far beyond the hundreds of peasant rebellions it caused. In 1921, a drought that in some Russian provinces formerly would have created no more than a minor famine instead triggered one of the worst famines of modern times—more than thirty million people faced starvation.

Confronted with a calamity that could threaten the survival of Communism, the party began providing some aid to the starving while urgently requesting international help. International relief, particularly from the United States through the American Relief Administration (ARA), was soon forthcoming. But even in the face of this historic disaster, Lenin wielded aid and food as a socialist weapon. Said Lenin—exemplifying what I mean by a thug regime, without an iota of compassion for the victims—"It is necessary to supply with food out of the state funds only those employees who are actually needed under conditions of maximum productivity of labor, and to distribute the food provisions by making the whole matter an instrumentality of politics, used with the view of cutting down on the number of those who are not absolutely necessary and to spur on those who are really needed."

Although there were agricultural dislocations caused by civil war, Lenin and the Communist Party were mainly responsible for some five million people starving to death or dying from associated diseases. The toll would have been much higher had not the ARA provided about $45,000,000 in aid (about $474,000,000 in 2002 dollars) to keep alive about ten million people.

STALIN'S COMMAND ECONOMY

Lenin's nationalization of workers and peasants was not the worse the Russian people would suffer. That would be the fruit of Stalin's tyranny. After Lenin's death from a stroke in 1924, there was a struggle for party rule between Leon Trotsky, commissar for war and Lenin's heir apparent, and Josef Stalin, general secretary of the Central Committee of the party. By 1928, Stalin had won the battle as to whether he or Trotsky would control the Communist Party. He now had full command over the Red Army, the secret police, and the Communist cadre, and he could carry out his plans to fully socialize what was now known as the Soviet Union. He especially intended to go much further than Lenin had dared go with the peasants, and he began to nationalize—without compensation—independent farms, their livestock, and their land and to consolidate them all into huge farm factories run by the party. Each farmer was to become an employee earning a daily wage for his work. It was to be total collectivization of the peasantry.

The peasants resisted, of course, and killed their animals rather than give them up, burned down their homes, fled to the cities, fired on the troops who came to enforce the party's commands, and committed suicide. This Peasant War destroyed and depopulated whole villages.

As it turned out, once the peasants "voluntarily" turned all they owned over to a collective farm or commune, they found these farms to be more like penal colonies. Party functionaries in Moscow commanded commune work and activity, usually from thousands of miles away. They regimented the life and daily routine of each commune member, although they knew nothing of local conditions and farming. Peasants, now commune "workers," had to obey orders without question, or Communist agents, spies, or their supervisors would report them.

This Peasant War was the largest and most deadly war fought between the two world wars, and yet it never appears on any list of wars during the twentieth century. Stalin also formally declared war on "wealthy" landowners, called kulaks. Party activists and even everyday workers became convinced that the kulaks were wholly responsible for the resistance to collectivization and its associated violence. Party officials throughout the Soviet Union spewed hate propaganda and consistently harangued activists on kulak evildoing. Whipped into a frenzy of hostility, activists and cadres who were sent out to the countryside in waves of collectivization unleashed their pent-up rage on any kulaks, who were regarded more as vermin than people.

This meant execution for many or a slow death in a labor camp. Others were barely more fortunate to be deported to forced settlements in remote regions like Siberia, which in some ways were worse than the labor camps.

This kind of scapegoating, deception, propaganda, and use of naked force is intrinsic to a command economy. To command an economy means just that: to use commands that subjects must obey absolutely—or else face prison, a labor camp, or death—to accomplish what is planned. Since human beings have their own interests and are unwilling to be used as the bricks and mortar to construct a utopia, they have to be persuaded or pushed, and as Communist cadres everywhere seemed to say, "If some die in the process, so be it—you can't make an omelet without breaking a few eggs."

In actuality, the liquidated kulaks were mainly the peasants who had been successful farmers—they owned fatter cows, they built better houses or barns, and they earned more than their neighbors. They were not overly rich (the average kulak earned less than the average factory worker or the rural official who was persecuting him) or exploiting landlords. They were simply the best farmers. And they paid for their success. The Peasant War consumed their lives and the country.

Speaking with Winston Churchill during a World War II summit, Stalin admitted that this Peasant War was worse than that against the Nazis. It "was a terrible struggle. . . . It was fearful." After saying that he had to deal with ten million kulaks, Stalin claimed that "the great bulk was very unpopular and was wiped out by their laborers."

Stalin's estimate was not far off. From 1929 to 1935, the party deported to labor camps or resettlements (usually to a slow death), possibly ten million, maybe even fifteen million kulaks and their families. These deportations included even infants, children, the elderly, and the infirm. Apparently, they stood in the way of progress, obstructing Stalin's collectivization. The cost in lives? The Soviets admitted that their collectivization and dekulakization campaigns might have killed five million to ten million peasants. This was mass murder, a hidden holocaust that few in the world outside the former Soviet Union knew about. All to apply an untested theoretical economic model of a command economy—Marxism-Leninism.

Did collectivization work? No. This greatest of experiments in scientific, social engineering utterly failed. It denied the laws of economics, human nature, and the free market. And so the communes never produced enough food for the Soviet population. The party had to resort to massive food imports and to giving the communes some freedom, but all to no avail. Stalin helped agricultural productivity most when he permitted the peasants, during their time off, to plant food on little plots of land the party gave them near their collectives. As one might expect, these little plots became highly productive and eventually accounted for most of the food produced in the Soviet Union, strongly vindicating the free-market model.

MAO TSE-TUNG'S COMMAND ECONOMY

In 1949, the Communist Party under Mao Tse-tung won the civil war against the Nationalist government and gained control over mainland China. Immediately, Mao moved to consolidate and centralize power, destroy all opposition, and make Communist authority supreme throughout the land, and—he hoped—make himself a world power. Acceptance, if not outright loyalty, had to be assured to apply the Communist economic model, especially among the mass of peasants.

This preparatory softening up and totalization of Chinese society took almost four years. It involved many movements and campaigns, each an effort by the new rulers to define specific goals and identify enemies. Millions were murdered in the process. Perhaps the best known of these movements was that of land reform. Acting through the party's organization, officials, and cadre, the method Mao used to destroy China's free agricultural market was simple: adopt every possible measure to rouse the hatred of the people and excite them into frenzy and hysterical animosity against the landlords.

Amid cadre-led cries of "enemy of the people" or "counterrevolutionary jackal" or "imperialist lackey," they would force their victims to face their "jury" with their hands tied and, with prompting from the "tribunal," recite their crimes against the revolution. Then a member of the tribunal would announce that the victims' punishment should be death, at which the coached jury would shout, "Death!" Then the cadre would immediately shoot the victims or wait until after they had dug their own graves.

The party officially ended land reform in 1953. According to the party, the movement affected around 480,000,000 of about 500,000,000 peasants; almost 114,000,000 acres forcibly changed hands. Under this guise of redistributing the land to the peasants, the party destroyed the power base of the gentry and rich peasants and received the acquiescence, if not the support, of the poorer peasants. In the process, about 4,500,000 landlords and relatively rich and better-off peasants were murdered.

With power now tightly centralized, society totally under control, and all possible countervailing forces destroyed or weakened—and now with a true command economy to work with (and having learned nothing from Stalin's horrible agricultural debacle)—Mao instituted collectivization. After some preliminary collectivization of the peasants into cooperatives, in April 1958, Mao began the forced collectivization of peasants into communes everywhere. The newly acquired land and all else the peasants owned—such as farming tools and even houses—became the property of the communes. Virtually all that hundreds of millions of peasants owned was nationalized in one titanic gulp.

The peasants were now the property of the commune, to labor like factory workers in teams and brigades at whatever the party commanded, to eat in common mess halls, and often to sleep together in barracks. In an instant, for about one-seventh of humanity, Mao destroyed family lives, traditions, personal property, privacy, personal initiative, and individual freedom. Mao and party functionaries now dictated every condition of the lives of the peasants, truly creating a command agricultural economy.

As this was going on, Mao also sought to catch up with the West in industrialization, particularly with Great Britain in steel production. He wanted to be a world leader and eventually, in is own words, to rule the world. He thought it would take fifteen years to achieve these goals.

Beginning in May 1958, slogans, exhortations, and drum-beating mass meetings mobilized the whole country in a "Great Leap Forward." The party hastily built workshops and factories and erected iron smelters throughout the countryside—one million by October, involving one hundred million Chinese. Officials ordered the communes and "encouraged" millions of urban families to contribute pots, pans, cutlery, and other iron and steel possessions for smelting. Peasants had to work day and night, fourteen or sixteen hours or more a day, on these projects. Production statistics zoomed, but top party officials soon realized that most local authorities had falsified their statistics. What factories and workshops produced was often worthless; much of the iron produced in backyard furnaces was impure and unusable slag.

All of this demolished Chinese living conditions. Daily food production fell to such an extent that each person had only 340 grams (12 ounces) of food per day. Considering the better rations of officials, soldiers, and agents, the ordinary person received less than 320 grams, as refugees reported, or less than half the normal daily calories needed. Predictably, in 1956 and 1957, famine struck in certain districts.

Add to this the many Chinese who were murdered by the party during this collectivization period. According to the best estimates, the collectivization and the Great Leap Forward, as well as campaigns against "rightists," probably cost an additional 5,550,000 Chinese lives.

THE ECONOMIC MIRACLES OF JAPAN, GERMANY, AND OTHERS

Look at the economic miracles in Germany and Japan. During World War II, the Allied bombing of these countries thoroughly destroyed their economies and infrastructures. Germany and Japan also had to absorb millions of returning soldiers and civilians, which for West Germany alone was about eight million ethnic and Reich Germans, most homeless and hungry. How did these countries recover as fast as they did, going from being among the most devastated nations in 1945 to being among the most economically powerful states in the early 1990s? In each case, this transformation was due to the effects of democratic freedom, particularly a free market.

For further proof, note the rapid economic growth and modernization of now-democratic South Korea. A good measure of this growth is its annual total of goods and services, or gross domestic product. From 1950 to 1985, this averaged a growth rate of 5.3 percent annually, despite the devastating Korean War from 1950 to 1953. For the world as a whole, the average was less than half that, or 2.3 percent. In 2004, South Korea's growth rate was even higher, at 4.8 percent, and it is now becoming a close competitor to Japan.

Compare this to North Korea, which has the same ethnicity, culture, and traditions and had a more developed industrial base before the communist takeover. While the South is prospering, the North—under a command economy—is bankrupt and economically ravaged, with its people suffering a severe famine and dying in the millions.

There is also the example of now-democratic Taiwan, whose economy from 1950 to 1985 grew at a rate of 7 percent, leveling off at 4.8 percent in 2004. Taiwan now is among the industrially developed nations. Then there is the "Asian tiger" that is Singapore, whose authoritarian government has allowed the market to be free; it has become an economic jewel of Southeast Asia. From 1950 to 1985, it grew at an average annual rate of 7.9 percent, making it the economically fastest growing country in the world. Hong

Kong, formerly under British rule, was another free market and economic jewel; since Communist China took it over from Britain by treaty in 1997, it remains to be seen how long this will last. Situated on a series of small islands and a small strip of mainland China, Hong Kong comprises only 397 square miles. In 1945, it had a population of fewer than six hundred thousand, but through natural population growth and by absorbing millions of refugees fleeing Communist China, its population swelled to more than six million. Despite the many people on this small bit of land, there was little unemployment; it had a bustling, productive, and continually growing economy and an annual growth rate of 6.9 percent up to 1997, which was only slightly behind Singapore and Taiwan at the time.

Now compare the results of the freedom in South Korea, Taiwan, Singapore, and Hong Kong to what happened in mainland China when Mao deprived its people of any freedom: total economic disaster, rebellions, economic retrogression, and tens of millions of people starving to death.

6

FREEDOM'S MORAL GOODS: NO FAMINE EVER

To FURTHER PROVE THAT to deny people freedom is to produce an economy of scarcity, famine, and death, note the wide-scale famines that Communist Parties also have made elsewhere. There is a continuing hunger in Communist and bankrupt North Korea during which about three million people died in the late 1990s. In an entirely different part of the world, communist Ethiopia placed controls over agricultural production in the 1980s, and one million Ethiopians starved to death or died from connected diseases—out of a population of 33.5 million people—which made this famine proportionally nearly as large as China's.

These empirical economic experiments with an alternative theoretical model to the free market, this incredibly bloody rebuilding of whole societies and cultures to match utopian plans, this forced fitting of people into one job or another, and this effort to do better by a dictator's command what free people can do for themselves has totally failed. Think of the marketplace in any liberal democracy compared to the shortages, long lines, limited choices, massive famines, and bloody repression that prevailed in these command economies. Better yet, think of the success of Bill Gates and Microsoft. There is a joke Eastern Europeans made about the command economy when they lived under communism: were a communist country to take over the Sahara Desert, we would hear nothing for ten years, after which there would be a shortage of sand.

Famines have also happened in authoritarian and fascist nations, although they were not even close in the resultant number of deaths to those under communism. By contrast, no democratically free people have ever had a famine. None. See, for example, Table 6.1 below.

TABLE 6.1
Twentieth-Century Famine Totals

	Free	Partly Free	Unfree	Colonies	Totals
Number of Countries	0	15	30[†]	16	61
Famine Dead (in 100,000s)	0	14,374	>60,080	>12,115	>86,569

*Freedom rating from Freedom House
[†] Angola 1974–76 famine counted in both unfree and colony categories

This is so important that I will put an even sharper point on it.

By the very nature of freedom, a free people are immune to one of humanity's worst disasters: famine.

THE GREAT AMERICAN DUST BOWL.

Democracies are not free of famines because nature is kinder to them. Note, for example, that in 1931, the worst drought ever to hit the United States began in the midwestern and southern plains states and centered on Colorado, Kansas, New Mexico, Oklahoma, and Texas. By 1934, the drought had spread to twenty-seven states and covered more than 75 percent of the country. Without rain, farmlands that had been overplowed and overgrazed became powder dry, resulting in huge dust storms called "black blizzards." Drought took out of cultivation about 35 million acres of farmland, and dust storms were removing topsoil from an additional 225 million acres. In 1935 alone, 850 million tons of topsoil probably blew off the southern plains.

As the drought and dust storms continued year after year, whole farm families fled in caravans, wagons, and carts piled high with belongings, leaving behind vacant homes and farm machinery partly buried in dusty soil. Through a variety of relief, cultivation, and conservation projects and programs, Congress and the Roosevelt administration acted to help farmers survive the drought, saving what land, crops, and livestock they could. Finally, in 1939, the rains came and the drought was over. While even lesser droughts had caused many tens of millions to starve to death where governments forbade a free market, I could not find a reference to even one American who starved to death during the Dust Bowl. Some Americans did die of suffocation in the dust storms, however, and some died of related diseases.

THE IRISH FAMINE

The worst famine to hit a European country in the last two centuries was the Irish famine from 1845 to 1849, which is sometimes blamed on a free market. A fungus attacked and destroyed the potato crop, the major cash crop of Ireland's peasants, causing massive famine throughout the country and the deaths of perhaps one million people, almost 13 percent of the population.

Now, Great Britain politically united with Ireland through the 1801 Act of Union, and before that, the Brits had ruled Ireland as, in effect, a colony. Over the previous centuries, the British had tightly controlled the development of the Irish economy through many repressive laws, many of which inhibited world and British trade with Ireland. In particular, various British governments were intent on suppressing Roman Catholicism, the religion of virtually all Irish peasants. Dating from 1695, and not fully repealed until 1829, laws to this end had a disastrous effect on Ireland's agriculture.

For example, the British forbade Irish Catholics to receive an education, engage in trade or commerce, vote, buy land, lease land, rent land above a certain worth, reap any profit from land greater than a third of their rent, and own a horse worth more than a certain value. This code so distorted Ireland's agricultural system, so impoverished the peasants, making them so dependent on their landlords, that any natural disaster affecting their crops could only result in a major famine. Moreover, because of limits on the franchise, the secret ballot, and the manner of representation and legislative voting, Great Britain was not even an electoral democracy at the time of the famine. It did not become a democracy until it democratized its electoral system later in the century.

MAO'S GREATEST FAMINE EVER

Mao's grandest, most ambitious, most destructive social engineering project ever—the total communization and nationalization of China's agriculture system, which involved more than half a billion human beings in its reduction to military-like central planning and administration through his vast and hurried "Great Leap Forward"—destroyed his nation's agricultural system. His program reduced food production to starvation levels. But since these policies were driven by Mao's lust for power, he refused to change them, and worse, he took what little food there was from the people to export to the third world, the Soviet Union, and Eastern Europe. With his people's life-saving food, he tried to buy influence, weapons, and heavy industrial factories. Thus, during the late 1950s and early 1960s, nearly 38 million people starved to death. As a comparison to this massive mountain of dead, it would be as though every man, women, and child in Arizona, Louisiana, Maryland, Missouri, Tennessee, Washington, and Wisconsin died of starvation.

Mao was forced to end the famine in 1962 when the Communist party rebelled and, against his wishes, ended the commune system, the Great Leap Forward, and food exports. Famine added to privation had been enough for some people. During 1961 and the following year, southern China experienced continuous guerrilla warfare, and Fukien Province, across from Taiwan, was the scene of a serious armed uprising. A former army officer led some eight thousand peasants to attack the militia and loot the granaries in Wuhua. Official sources admit that, during 1961 alone, resistance included 146,852 granary raids, 94,532 arsons, and 3,738 revolts. In addition, according to General Hsieh Fu-chih, the minister of security, 1,235 party and administrative cadres were assassinated.

• • •

The evidence thus overwhelmingly supports freedom as a means to the economic betterment of society and the fulfillment of human needs. See, for example, Table 6.2 below.

TABLE 6.2
Wealth and Prosperity for 190 Nations by
Level of Freedom, 1997–98

	Free	Partly Free	Unfree
Average Freedom Level*	13	8	3
Average Purchasing Power Parity per Person[†]	11,918	4,285	3,733
Average Human Poverty Index[‡]	14	26	34
Average Human Development Index[§]	0.8	0.63	0.58

*Combined rating of Freedom House on civil liberties and political rights, which varies from a rating of 2 to 14. For this table, free = ratings of 11–14, partly free = 6–10, unfree = 2–5.

[†] Purchasing power parity per person is the average person's ability in dollars to purchase goods comparable to what can be purchased by those living in other states. This is a good measure of comparable average wealth (based on data for 1998).

[‡] Source: United Nations Development Program (based on data for 1998).

[§] The Human Development Index comprises life expectancy at birth, adult literacy, gross primary, secondary, and tertiary enrollment, and GNP per capita in purchasing power parity and is taken from the United Nations Development Program (based on data for 1998).

Quite simply,

Freedom produces wealth and prosperity.

This is a moral good of freedom, a moral reason for people to be free. I have argued that people have an inherently moral right to be free, regardless of the consequences of freedom—its utility. Now we can say that freedom has very desirable, moral consequences for humanity: wealth and prosperity. This may be the most important moral good of freedom, but it is not the only one. Freedom has yet other moral goods, and of these, not many people are aware.

7

FREEDOM'S MORAL GOODS: MINIMIZING POLITICAL VIOLENCE

RIOTS, COUPS, REVOLUTIONS, BLOODY demonstrations, communal violence, terrorism, suicide bombings, rebellions, insurrections, unrest, and turmoil are the stuff of our daily newspapers. The one common ingredient for all this bloody internal violence is that the people who usually suffer from it also must endure being partially or totally enslaved. Liberal democracies have little internal political violence. There is a strong inverse correlation here.

> The more democratic freedom a people have,
> the less severe their internal political violence.

This is a statistical fact, easily verified by noting where and under what kind of government such violence occurs. See, for example, Table 7.1 on page 64. That freedom minimizes such violence does not necessarily mean that freedom ends it, however. Some rioting, civil strife, terrorism, and even civil war might still occur in a democracy. But we

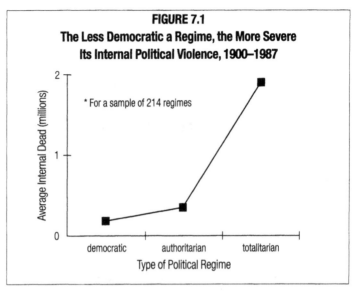

FIGURE 7.1
The Less Democratic a Regime, the More Severe Its Internal Political Violence, 1900–1987

* For a sample of 214 regimes

Average Internal Dead (millions)

Type of Political Regime

democratic authoritarian totalitarian

know that we can sharply reduce such violence, on the average, to the mildest and smallest amount possible, through democratic freedom.

How do we understand this power of democratic freedom? Many believe that the answer to this is psychological and personal. They think that free societies educate people against the mass killing of their neighbors; that free people are not as belligerent as those elsewhere; that free people have deep inhibitions against killing others; and that free people are more tolerant of their differences. There is much truth in all this, but commentators often neglect the social preconditions of this psychological resistance to political violence. The answer is that:

> The social structure of a free, democratic society
> creates the psychological conditions
> for its greater internal peace.

64

Freedom's Moral Goods: Minimizing Political Violence

Where freedom flourishes, there are relatively free markets and freedom of religion, association, ideas, and speech. Corporations, partnerships, associations, societies, leagues, churches, schools, and clubs proliferate. Through free people's interests, work, and play, they become members of these multiple groups, each a separate pyramid of power, each competing with the others and with their government for their membership, time, and resources.

Similarly, in a free society, the critical social distinctions of wealth, power, and prestige are subdivided in many ways. Few people are high on all three. More are low on all three, but these people are not close to a majority. Most people have different amounts of wealth, power, and prestige. Even Bill Gates, while the highest on wealth, does not have the prestige of a popular movie actor or musician or the power of a judge.

All this pluralism in their group memberships and in wealth, power, and prestige cross-pressures people's interests and motivations. For all free people across a society, there is a constantly changing intersection of interests and differences.

Because of all these diverse connections and linkages in a democratic society, politicians, leaders, and groups have a paramount interest in keeping the peace. And where a conflict might escalate into violence, as over some religious or environmental issue, people's interests are so cross-pressured by different groups and ties that they simply cannot develop the needed depth of feeling and single-minded devotion to any interest at stake, except perhaps to their families and children.

Yet there is something else about a democratically free society that is even more important than these violence-reducing links and cross-pressures: their culture. Where people are free, as in a free market, exchange dominates and resolves conflicts. "You scratch my back, and I'll scratch yours." "You give me that, and I'll give you this." Money is often the currency of such exchange, but also exchanged are privileges, benefits, positions, and so on.

In a democracy, people soak up certain norms governing their conflicts. They tolerate their differences, negotiate some compromise, and in the process, they make concessions to one another. From the highest government official to the lowest worker, from the consideration of bills in a legislature to who does the dishes after dinner, there is bargaining of one sort or another going on to resolve an actual or potential conflict. Some of this becomes regularized, as in the bargaining of unions and management in the United States as structured by the Labor Relations Board, or the tradition in some families that dictates that the wife will always wash the dishes. But so much more involves bargaining.

Therefore, in a free society, a culture of bargaining—what one might call an exchange or democratic culture—evolves. This is part of the settling in that takes place when a nation first becomes democratic. Authoritarian practices—doing things through orders, decrees, and commands sent down through a hierarchy—gradually gets replaced by many hierarchies of power and the use of bargaining and its techniques of negotiation and compromise to settle conflicts. Free people soon come to expect that when they have a conflict, they will negotiate the issues and resolve it through concessions and the splitting of differences. The more years a democracy exists, the more its people's expectations become hardened into social customs and perception. No matter the conflict, people who have long been democratically free do not expect revolution and civil war. For, most important, they see one another as democratic, as part of one's in-group, one's moral, democratic universe. They each share not only socially—in overlapping groups, functions, and linkages—but also in culture.

This structure of freedom, this "spontaneous society," serves to inhibit violence, to culturally dispose people to cooperation, negotiation, compromise, and tolerance. Consider the acceptance and application of the U.S. Constitution and congressional rules in settling that most serious of political conflicts in 1999—whether President Bill Clinton would be fired from office—and the even more potentially violent, month-long dispute over the outcome of the 2000 presidential election. These supremely contentious disputes, these most potentially violent issues, were decided with no loss of life, no injuries, no destruction of property, no disorder, and no political instability.

But this is, so to speak, one end of the stick. This spontaneous society explains why a free people are most peaceful in their national affairs, but why should those societies in which people are commanded by absolute dictators or a gang of thugs—where people are most unfree—be the most violent? The worst of these dictators rule their people and organize their society according to ideological or theological imperatives. Be it Marxism-Leninism and the drive for true communism—as in the Russian Revolution, socialist egalitarianism as in Burma, racial purity as in Nazi Germany, or the realization of God's will as in Iran—the dictators operate through a rigid and society-wide command structure. And this polarizes society.

First, the competing pyramids of power—church, schools, businesses, and so on—that discipline, check, and balance each other and government in a free society do not exist. There is one pyramid of power, with the dictator or ruling elite at the top, with various levels of government in the middle and near the bottom, and with the mass of enslaved subjects at the bottom.

Second, where in a free society separate cross-cutting groups service diverse interests, there is now, in effect, only one division in society: that between those thugs in power who command and those who must obey. In the worst of these nations, such as Pol Pot's Cambodia, Kim Il-sung's North Korea, Stalin's Soviet Union, and Mao's China, the people could only work for the party, buy food from its stores, read newspapers it publishes, see only its movies and television programs, go to its schools, study its textbooks, and pray at a church it controls, if it allows any of this at all. In Cambodia, no churches, money, newspapers, movies and television, or schools were permitted.

These restrictions sharply divide society into those in power and those out of power—into them versus us. This aligns the vital interests of us versus them along one conflict fault line traversing society, as a magnet aligns metal filings along its magnetic forces. Any minor gripe about the society or politics is against the same "them," and when one says "they" are responsible for a problem or conflict, friends and loved ones know exactly who is meant—the whole apparatus of the dictator's rule: his henchmen, police, officials, spies, and bureaucrats.

Since this regime owns and runs nearly everything, any minor issue becomes a matter of the dictator's power, legitimacy, or credibility. A strike in a small town against a government-owned factory is a serous matter to the dictator. Such a strike may be symbolic for the people, a display of resistance they should support, and if the dictator shows weakness in defense of his policies, no matter how localized, the strike can spread along the "us versus them" fault line and crystallize into a nationwide rebellion. So the dictator must use massive force to quash dissent. The regime cannot afford to let any resistance, any display of independence, anywhere in the country by anybody, go unchallenged. Even a peaceful demonstration, like those in Burma and China, must be violently squashed, with the leaders arrested, tortured for information, and often killed.

So rule is by the gun, and violence is its natural accompaniment. But there is more to this. As a culture of accommodation is a consequence of freedom, a culture of force and violence is a consequence of dictatorial rule. Where such rule is absolute, this is also a culture of fear, perhaps in the worst of these thugdoms, shivering fear—the result of not knowing when another might perceive something one is doing as wrong and report it to the police; not knowing whether authorities will consider one's ancestry or race or religion reason for persecution; not knowing about the safety of one's loved ones, who may be dragged off to serve in the military, disappear because of something they said, or be made into some sexual plaything.

The fear exists up and down the dictator's command structure as well. The secret police may shoot a general because of his joke about the leader, or they may jail and torture top government functionaries because of a rumored plot. The dictator himself must always fear that his security forces will turn their guns on him.

The less free a society and the more coercive the
commands that dominate it, the greater the

> polarization and culture of fear and violence and the
> more likely extreme violence will occur.

I argued previously that by promoting wealth and prosperity, freedom is a moral good. Here, I have pointed out that freedom also promotes nonviolence and peace within a nation. This is also a moral good of freedom. It is another moral reason why people should be democratically free.

LENIN'S RED TERROR AND PEASANT WAR

Originally the left wing of the Russian Social Democratic Labor Party (Lenin's Bolsheviks) was a small, uncompromising, and militant group of dedicated Marxist communists. Their incredibly small number, considering subsequent events, was clear when the first all-Russian Congress of Soviets was held, and only 105 out of 1,090 delegates declared themselves as Bolsheviks.

In November 1917, with the powerful Petrograd garrison remaining neutral, Lenin seized the Winter Palace in Petrograd. Since this was the seat of Alexander Kerensky's shaky provisional government that had caused the czar to abdicate, and Kerensky had only 1,500 to 2,000 defenders, the 6,000 to 7,000 soldiers, sailors, and Red Guards thrown together by Lenin's Bolsheviks easily overthrew the government. Widely unpopular, however, and faced with strong political opposition, Lenin at first made common cause with the Left Social Revolutionaries, a militant socialist group, in order to survive, centralize power, and consolidate this communist revolution. In 1919, Lenin adopted the name Communist Party for the Bolsheviks and their political allies.

To fight this forceful takeover of the government, generals throughout the Russian empire created whole armies—some led by anti-Russians and nationalists, some by anti-communists, some by pro-monarchists or pro-authoritarians, some by advocates of democracy. These so-called White armies were a direct threat to the new Communist Party and its so-called Red Army. Moreover, in the areas controlled by the communists, the clergy, bourgeoisie, and professionals opposed them. The urban workers, who had been communist allies at first, also soon turned against them when they saw that the communists had taken over the soviets (elected governing councils) and would not yield power to the worker unions or representatives. Peasants, who had also been especially supportive when the communists began to give them land taken from rich landowners and the aristocrats' estates, turned to outright rebellion when the communists began forcibly requisitioning their grain and produce.

In the first eighteen months of Lenin's rule, in twenty provinces alone, there were 344 peasant rebellions. Up to early 1921, there were about 50 anti-communist rebel armies. White armies and peasant rebellions aside, even in the urban industrial areas, communist control was precarious at best. What saved Lenin and the party was their "Red Terror."

By 1918, Lenin had ordered the wide use of terror, including inciting workers to murder their "class enemies." Mass shootings, arrests, and torture were an integral part of covert communist policy, not simply a reaction to the formation of the White armies. Indeed, the Red Terror preceded the start of the civil war.

Lenin directed the terror against "enemies of the people" and "counter-revolutionaries," which he defined primarily by social group and class membership: bourgeoisie, aristocrats, "rich" landowners (kulaks), and clergy. Communists jailed actual or ideologically defined opponents, tortured many barbarously to force them to sign false confessions, and executed large numbers of them. They shot many men and women out of hand: 200 in this jail, 450 in that prison yard, 320 in the woods outside of town. Even in small outlying areas, such as the small Siberian town of Ossa Ochansk, they massacred 3,000 men in 1919. This went on and on. As late as 1922, the communists executed 8,100 priests, monks, and nuns. This alone is equivalent to a modern jumbo passenger plane crashing, with no survivors, each day for thirty-two days.

Moreover, the communists showed no mercy to prisoners taken in battle with the White armies and often executed them. They even shot the relatives of defecting officers, as when the Eighty-sixth Infantry Regiment went over to the Whites in March 1919—the communists killed all the relatives of each defecting officer. Places reoccupied after the defeat of one White army or another suffered systematic bloodbaths; the Cheka screened through the population for aristocrats, bourgeoisie, and supporters of the Whites. When defeated one White general fled with his remaining officers and men from the Crimea, the Red Army and Cheka may have slaughtered from 50,000 to 150,000 people during reoccupation of the area.

Then there was the Peasant War, which, although it tends to be ignored, was no less vicious than the civil war. Under the guise of requisitioning food, communists tried to plunder village after village, which understandably resulted in pitched battles, massacres, and frequent atrocities. Twenty-six major uprisings began in July 1918; in August, forty-seven; in September, thirty-five. The communists fiercely fought the Peasant War over the full length and breadth of the new Soviet Union from 1918 through 1922, and at any one time, there were apparently more than one hundred rebellions involving thousands of peasant fighters.

About 500,000 people were killed in this Peasant War, half in combat and the other half murdered by the communists. The number of combat deaths in the civil and peasant wars—rather than those resulting from mass murder—was likely about 1,350,000 people. Although a fantastic toll by normal standards, this was a fraction of the total killed during this period.

By 1920, Lenin and the Communist Party had surely won the civil war. And through the Red Terror, they secured the home front. The terror eliminated or cowed the opposition and enabled Lenin to stabilize the party's control, assure its continuity and authority, and above all, save communism. Lenin bought this success at a huge cost in lives. My conservative estimate is that about 500,000 people, including at least 200,000 officially executed, were murdered, which should be added to the probable 250,000 murdered in the Peasant War.

8

ON FREEDOM'S MORAL GOODS: ELIMINATING DEMOCIDE

BY SHOOTING, DROWNING, BURYING alive, stabbing, beating, crushing, torture, suffocation, starvation, exposure, poison, and countless other ways that lives can be wiped out, dictators have killed unarmed and helpless people. Intentionally. With forethought. This is murder. It is *democide*.

> In the twentieth century, governments murdered, as a prudent estimate, 272,000,000 men, women, and children. It could be over 400,000,000.

The absolutely incredible number of murders carried out by governments—often as policy decided by ruling thugs—is largely unknown. Were people, even the most educated people, asked to estimate the number of people murdered by governments in the last century, they probably would suggest ten million. Maybe even twenty million. But this is much too low.

The more popularly understood term for government murder is genocide, but there is a difference between democide and genocide that must be recognized. In short:

- *Democide* is a government's murder of people for any or no reason at all.
- *Genocide* is the murder of people because of their race, ethnicity, religion, nationality, or language.

The most infamous example of genocide is Nazi Germany's cold-blooded murder of nearly 5,300,000 Jews during World War II. Many people incorrectly believe that was the only major case of government murder. But there was also Mao's murder of 77,000,000 Chinese, Stalin's murder of 42,672,000 Russians, Hitler's murder of 20,946,000 (including the Jews), Chiang Kai-shek's murder of 10,214,000, Lenin's murder of 4,017,000, Tojo's murder of 3,990,000, Pol Pot's murder of 2,397,000, Khan's (Yahya of Pakistan) murder of 1,500,000, and Tito's murder of 1,172,000.

The overall, obscene toll of 272 million people murdered is as though the world had suffered a nuclear war with the deaths and destruction spread over the century. There is a good reason that all this killing is unknown. The authoritarian and totalitarian thug regimes that do most of the killing usually control who writes their histories and what appears in them. Also, democratically free people project onto the rest of the world their own democratic cultural biases. They see governments as doing good things for their people. Some policies may be wrong, some stupid, but the idea of murdering people because of their politics, religion, or ethnicity or by quota is alien—except, of course, for what those evil Nazis did to the Jews.

Then there is the problem of digesting or getting a feel for what a million murdered—not to mention 272 million—means. To get a sense for just one hundred thousand dead, think of laying these corpses head to toe. Assume—since many were babies, young children, and short adults—that each corpse averages a little more than five feet long. The line of one hundred thousand bodies would stretch almost one hundred miles long. This example provides a simple multiplier: two hundred thousand bodies would stretch head to toe for nearly two hundred miles; a million murdered would be almost a thousand miles. Maybe now you can feel how incredible, how horrible it is that one hundred thousand or even one thousand human beings—each a separate soul, each with a unique personality and emotions, each a thinking, feeling human being—would have their lives wiped out. Each death leaves countless heartbroken loved ones, thus multiplying the toll. Human misery cannot be quantified in numbers, but numbers are necessary for recounting the sad tale of such gargantuan crimes.

RWANDA'S GREAT GENOCIDE

The Rwandan genocide of 1994 (known as the Great Genocide), though by far the largest in the country's history, was only one of many acts of genocide carried out by different Rwandan governments in the decades before 1994—and that have continued since. The Western media have greatly misunderstood the 1994 genocide as a tribal meltdown, as ethnic hatred and intolerance run amok. The mental picture is of a Hutu running wildly down a street, swinging a machete at any Tutsi he can catch. This is largely a myth.

Rather, the Great Genocide was a well-calculated mass murder planned by Hutu government leaders. Surely individual Hutus who hated Tutsis, or had grievances against certain Tutsis, joined in the blood-fest, and undoubtedly, sadistic Hutus saw this genocide as an excuse to kill. But we should not overlook the many Hutus who refused to kill and even protected Tutsis at the risk of their lives. This genocide was part of a political struggle to maintain power, as was the "ethnic cleansing" that happened later in Bosnia and Kosovo. It exemplified the iron law of human behavior: power kills.

Rwandan President Juvenal Habyarimana's government allowed virtually no freedom. He created a one-party state with the intention of controlling and mobilizing the population. The government divided people into communes, and any citizen who wanted to move in or out of an assigned commune had to report to the police. All citizens had to register, and as in Burma, the government forced everyone to do a certain amount of forced labor: building roads, clearing brush, digging ditches, and so on. They also had to participate in weekly propaganda meetings to glorify the party.

In 1990, in the midst of Rwanda's economic troubles, Tutsi refugees who had fled the country when the Hutus seized power and began killing Tutsis, formed a political and military force they named the Front Patriotique Rwandais (FPR, sometimes called the RPF). FPR invaded the country but was defeated. It tried to hold on to parts of the country and periodically resumed its offensive until the government launched the 1994 genocide.

By April 1994, events had prepared the way for this mass killing. The economy was a mess, and tensions between Hutus and Tutsis were at a boiling point due to continuing FPR assaults. The country was so beleaguered that it began to look as though Habyarimana would surrender to foreign pressure and allow the Tutsis to share power. Radical Hutu elites and top governmental leaders, however, had other plans.

On April 6, 1994, a plane carrying Habyarimana and Burundian President Cyprien Ntaryamira crashed under mysterious circumstances. The prevailing theory was that Habyarimana's own presidential guard shot down the aircraft. Whether radical Hutus planned this assassination or not, it triggered the Great Genocide.

The government—that is, President Habyarimana's wife, a few close advisers, and three brothers-in-law—had prepared for the Great Genocide before Habyarimana's death. The midlevel organizers numbered about three hundred to five hundred officials and bureaucrats. The police, with a special Hutu militia (*interhamwe*) of 7,000 to 14,000 Tutsi-haters at their command, did the dirty work. Officials involved in the plan had specifically organized the militia to murder Tutsis, and they succeeded very well: some may well have killed as many as two hundred to three hundred people. Insiders had also trained a palace guard of about 6,000 Hutu to help the militia and exterminate Hutu and Tutsi political opponents and their supporters. Even Hutu moderates did not escape death.

As with the Holocaust, when Nazi killing squads were often led and composed of PhDs and other professionals, the claims of the powerful and authoritative easily swayed the well educated to murder. In the Great Genocide, Hutu lawyers, teachers, professors, medical doctors, journalists, and other professionals contributed to the methodical annihilation of Tutsis or defiant Hutus.

By June 6, eight weeks after it had begun, this deliberate Great Genocide had already taken some 500,000 Rwandan lives, mostly Tutsi. Whole families were massacred, including babies. As the Great Genocide progressed, the United Nations, Belgium, and particularly the United States showed extreme caution in using the word *genocide* to describe the action much less intervening to stop it. Even when the deliberate nature of the government's action became too blatant to ignore, the Clinton administration refused to call it genocide. To do so would have required foreign signatories of the Genocide Convention, including the United States, to immediately get involved. The Clinton administration also delayed in agreeing to the details of dispatching U.N. troops and prevented any foreign action until June 8, two months into the Great Genocide. Then, the Security Council finally received U.S. agreement and authorized troops to enter Rwanda and prevent further genocide. These troops backed the Tutsi FPR, helped defeat the Hutu conspirators, and caused their government to collapse. An FPR-backed government then took power and installed a dictatorship as severe as the one it replaced.

POL POT'S KILLING FIELDS

The incredible killing that took place in Cambodia from 1975 to 1979 is an example of large-scale, nongenocidal mass murder and only secondarily one of genocide. This democide was part of an attempt by communists to impose a revolution on the country. They tried to abolish its religion, eradicate its culture, totally remodel its economy, communize all social interaction, and control all speech and writing. They exterminated anyone with any ties to Western nations or to Vietnam, Laos, and Thailand, and they eliminated everyone who had any connection to the previous government or military.

In proportion to its population, Pol Pot and the Khmer Rouge imposed on Cambodians a human catastrophe unequaled by any other country in the twentieth century. The country probably lost slightly less than four million people to war, rebellion, Khmer Rouge–made famine, and democide—genocide, nonjudicial executions, and massacres—or close to 56 percent of its 1970 population. Successive governments and guerrilla groups murdered almost 3.3 million men, women, and children—including thirty-five thousand foreigners—between 1970 and 1980. Most of these, probably as many as 2.4 million, were murdered by the communist Khmer Rouge both before and (to a much greater extent) during their takeover of Cambodia after April 1975.

The United States had supported and supplied the Cambodian military government of Gen. Lon Nol, but Congress ended all aid to him with the withdrawal of U.S. troops from Vietnam in 1973. After successive retreats, Lon Nol could no longer even defend the capital, Phnom Penh, against the Khmer Rouge guerrillas, and the Cambodian army was forced to declare a cease-fire and lay down its arms. On April 17, 1975, a ragtag bunch of solemn teenagers clad in black pajamas, red scarves, and Mao caps and carrying weapons of all kinds walked or were trucked from different directions into Phnom Penh.

But before the people could enjoy a few days of peace, the Khmer Rouge did the unimaginable: they turned their weapons on the two million to three million inhabitants of the capital. Shouting threats of immediate death, waving their weapons angrily, and actually shooting inhabitants, they demanded that everyone leave the city. In Phnom Penh and all other newly occupied cities and towns, their order to evacuate was absolute. The Khmer Rouge evicted nearly 4.25 million urban Cambodians and refugees—even the sick, infirm, and aged—from cities and towns into a largely unprepared countryside. Even for those on the operating table or in labor during childbirth, the order was unquestionable: "Go! Go! You must leave!"

Failure to evacuate meant death. Failure to begin evacuation promptly meant death. Failure of anyone to obey Khmer Rouge orders meant death. Failure to give the Khmer Rouge what they wanted—whether a car, motor scooter, bicycle, watch, or whatever—meant death.

The Khmer Rouge told the refugees to return to their home villages. But the urbanites were ordered to villages on the whim of the soldiers and cadres they encountered along the way. People were jumbled together, trudging for days or weeks, usually with only the clothes, coverings, and provisions they had snatched at the last moment. Many had minimal supplies, because the Khmer Rouge, to minimize disorder, had told them that the evacuation would be for only a few days. The very young and the very old and those already sick, injured, or infirm died on the roads or trails. And as the pitiful evacuees reached their homes or assigned villages, there was usually no relief from the terror and fear they had already endured. The situation was different only in kind.

The toll from this outrageous and bloody evacuation, including those killed outright, is in dispute. Whether 40,000 to 80,000 evacuees were murdered or died, as one scholar sympathetic to the Khmer Rouge claimed, or 280,000 to 400,000 died, as the CIA estimated, the sheer horror of this urban expulsion is undeniable.

Primarily, this evacuation was done as a matter of ideology. The Khmer Rouge saw the cities as the home of foreign ideas, capitalists, and bourgeoisie intellectuals; all of whom were believed to be thoroughly corrupt. The Cambodian citizenry required a thorough cleansing. And those whom the Khmer Rouge believed had been corrupted by city life—professionals, businesspeople, public officials, teachers, writers, and workers—must either be eliminated or reeducated and purified. To the Khmer Rouge, the best way to remake those "corrupted minds" that they allowed to survive was to make them work in the fields alongside pure peasants.

This inhuman expulsion was an opening salvo in the Khmer Rouge campaign to remake Cambodian culture and society in order to construct pure communism. It created a border-to-border, open-air concentration/forced-labor camp with rigid rules that made the people's lives worse, more controlled, and more dangerous than those of slaves. All peasants were collectivized and forced to labor on collective farms solely for the communist revolution. The Khmer Rouge forbade all political, civil, or human rights. They prohibited travel between villages without a pass. They forced Cambodians to eat and sleep in communes, and they ordered even young children to work in the fields. In some regions, everyone had to work from about 6:00 a.m. to 8:00 or 10:00 p.m., with time off only for "political education."

And these slaves were fed barely enough to keep them alive while further weakening their bodies through extreme malnutrition. They ate an average of 800 to 1,200 calories per day; for even light labor, a worker requires an average of 1,800 calories. Nor did the Khmer Rouge provide them with protection against exposure and disease. Even Pol Pot admitted in 1976 that 80 percent of the peasants had malaria.

The Khmer Rouge permanently closed all primary, secondary, and technical schools, as well as colleges and universities. They shut down all hospitals and murdered Western-trained medical doctors. They prohibited sex between unmarried individuals, and in some places, they threatened children with death for as little as holding hands. Unauthorized contact was forbidden even between those who were married—also at risk of death. Khmer Rouge allowed no appeals, no courts, no judges, no trials, and no law. They eliminated all money, businesses, books, and newspapers. They banned music. They eliminated practicing lawyers, doctors, teachers, engineers, scientists, and all other professionals, because whatever truths these professions possessed, "the peasant could pick up through experience."

Throughout Cambodia, quaking fear was a normal condition of life. The Khmer Rouge systematically massacred people because of past positions, associations, or relatives. When the cadre discovered top military men from the previous government, former government officials or bureaucrats, business executives, or high monks, they and their whole families (including babies) were murdered, sometimes after extended torture.

Similar slaughter often awaited those who had had any relations with the West or with Vietnam, the Soviet Union, or those who had ever opposed the Khmer Rouge. The Khmer Rouge were even known to execute people found with Western items (such as books), those who spoke French or English, or those who had been schooled beyond the seventh grade. In some areas, wearing eyeglasses was a capital offense.

Not only did the Khmer Rouge run amok while massacring their people, they also tried to destroy the heart of peasant life everywhere. Hinayana Buddhism had been a state religion, and the priesthood of saffron-robed monks was a central part of Cambodian culture. Some 90 percent of Cambodians observed some form of Buddhism. Many received a rudimentary schooling from the monks, and many young people became monks for part of their lives. The Khmer Rouge could not tolerate so powerful an institution and therefore set out to destroy it. They exterminated the leading monks and either murdered or defrocked the lesser ones.

In summary, the Cambodia of the Khmer Rouge was little more than a forced labor and death camp, and all citizens suffered the torments of hell.

In foreign relations, Pol Pot and his people hated their neighboring communist Vietnamese and felt no fraternal loyalty to them. They saw the Vietnamese as racially inferior and as the foremost danger to the Khmer Rouge revolution. It was not long after their victory that they began to attack Vietnamese territory. In many of these incursions they fought pitched battles with Vietnamese units, attacked and burned Vietnamese villages, and murdered Vietnamese peasants.

Vietnam did not long endure these attacks and finally launched a full-scale invasion of Cambodia. Her heavily armed troops, backed with gunships and tanks, easily rolled over the fewer, more lightly armed Khmer Rouge defenders. After a month of fighting, the invading Vietnamese occupied Phnom Penh.

Surviving Khmer Rouge, along with possibly one hundred thousand people they forced to move with them (vengefully killing many along the way), retreated to a mountainous region along the Thai border. From there and from refugee camps they soon controlled in Thailand, they launched a guerrilla war against the Vietnamese and the puppet Heng Samrin regime (which the Vietnamese set up to rule Cambodia) and then against the Vietnam-established Cambodian government when the Vietnamese withdrew from the country. Only in the last decade would the Khmer Rouge finally be defeated.

STALIN'S GREAT TERROR

Then there was Stalin—a megamurderer well beyond Hitler and only outdone by Mao. As I mentioned in chapter 5, once in power over the Soviet Union, Stalin collectivized the peasants in a bloody peasant war. He also forcibly starved to death five million Ukrainians. But the worst was yet to come.

By 1934, the peasant war was over. But it had left an aftertaste. Some activists and party officials in the field could not accept the horrors of the previous years with ideological equanimity. Shooting children as kulaks? Starving to death helpless old women? Was this what Marxism meant? Moreover, many old Bolsheviks who could contrast Bolshevik ideals with the present still had the old rebellious spirit.

There were the top contenders for Stalin's power, each with his own followers, each willing to criticize Stalin's policies and argue alternatives. Stalin ruled, but he did so with an increasingly shaky party beneath him and the real possibility of a palace coup. He did not rule securely. This was underlined in January 1934 at the Congress of the Communist Party of the Soviet Union. Most delegates were determined to replace Stalin; some wanted to replace him with Sergei Kirov, a popular member of the Politburo, head of the Leningrad Party, and a Russian—unlike Stalin.

Stalin was a man of action. He met this early challenge by confronting his opponents; in effect, launching a coup d'etat against the party. First, Kirov was assassinated. Then, under the guise of exposing the perpetrators of this abominable deed, Stalin set up special staffs of NKVD in every district executive committee of Leningrad to uncover who had been involved in the assassination (which turned out to be almost the whole committee, of course). The "conspirators" were shot or sent to labor camps. None could appeal. A quarter of Leningrad was purged—cleaned out—in 1934/35.

This bloody purge was extended to other major cities and eventually to the whole country. It reached its zenith with Stalin's appointment of a supreme headhunter, Nikolai Yezhov, as chief of the NKVD in 1936. Immediately justifying Stalin's faith in him, Yezhov inaugurated his reign by ordering the executions of all NKVD commissars in the republics, and also their deputies. No NKVD officer who had served under the former head, Genrikh Yagoda, was safe either. In 1937, three thousand of these were shot. As the murderous purge embraced one party bureau and then another, one government agency and then another, one social institution and then another, its nature, extent, and scope began to defy reason and belief.

Throughout the country, top and middle echelons of the party and government were executed or sent to camps to die. Their replacements, and sometimes even those who replaced these replacements, also were either subsequently murdered or sent to labor camps. Many old Bolsheviks and other top communists were arrested and tried before show trials, during which they confessed to spying, "counter-revolutionary" plotting, and other "crimes." All of them were sentenced to death. The chief of Soviet military intelligence was also shot. Military intelligence agents serving abroad were brought home and shot. Key Soviet officers and diplomats who had played a role in the Spanish Civil War were shot.

The top military echelons of the Red Army and Navy were shot. Marshal M. N. Tukhachevsky, the chief of staff, was shot along with seven high-ranking generals for plotting against the country (Tukhachevsky was posthumously exonerated in 1956). Overall, about half of the Red Army officer corps was shot or imprisoned—35,000 men. These included 3 of the 5 marshals, 13 out of 15 commanders, all 8 admirals, 220 out of 406 brigade commanders, 75 out of the 80 sitting on the supreme military council, all military district commanders, and all 11 vice commissars of war. Many had the status of Heroes of the Soviet Union—until their execution. There is no evidence that they plotted against Stalin, the party, the country, or even tried to use their commands to save themselves.

Not only were the officers, officials, and workers in the party or the government executed or sent to labor camps, often with an impossible twenty-five-year sentence, but they were accompanied by their wives, parents, children, and often their associates and friends. It was assumed that all those who were arrested and interrogated had to be part of a plot or conspiracy. NKVD interrogators labored over each prisoner (interrogators themselves could and were arrested for "wrecking" if they seemed insufficiently dedicated) to uncover other conspirators and dates—often these were supplied by the interrogators themselves. Sometimes the NKVD would murder people with no pretext—simply to meet a quota set by the party, which was the de facto government

How could this be? Top communists believed that a certain percentage of the population opposed the party and therefore had to be eliminated. But in typical communist fashion, this was not something that could be left to the discretion of a low-level cadre. After all, to ensure that low-level cadres were correctly guided in their work, the party had to put quotas on iron, steel, pigs, wheat, and virtually every element in the Soviet economy. It followed that officials should also be given quotas of people to murder. Furthermore, such thinking and practice were consistent with the communist idea of central planning and control. From NKVD headquarters in Moscow the order would go out to officials or the cadre in a village or town to kill so many "enemies of the people." Soon enough, the NKVD would receive word that it had been done.

The whole country came under an arrest quota; that is, orders were issued to arrest a specified percentage of the population. How many were arrested? About eight million people from mid-1936 through 1938. Possibly as many as fourteen million—about 9 percent of the population—were under NKVD detention. These were not all party members or officials; most were peasants and workers that had nothing to do with the party or with Stalin's power over the party. They had done nothing wrong. Yet they were arrested by the millions. Why?

Only one answer is plausible. There was a growing labor shortage, and since the NKVD needed more forced laborers for its enterprises, the NKVD developed a quota system to collect its slaves. Such an interpretation of the fact becomes even more plausible when one see that prisoners whose sentences were expiring—those who, against the odds, had managed to survive the deadly camp conditions—were given an additional ten-, fifteen-, or twenty-five-year sentence. This additional sentence would be announced, lacking further interrogation or hearing and based on nothing the prisoner had done, to the prisoner brigades when they were summoned to the administration building and then made to sign the paperwork.

The millions and millions of arrests during 1937–38 got out of hand. Interrogators were swamped, prison cells were stuffed with new arrivals, and the system was breaking down. In some places, faced with finding space for the daily crowd of newly arrested prisoners, officials had holes dug in the ground, a roof put over the top, then herded the prisoners into them. Small prisons teemed with thousands. A prison in Kharkov built for around 800 held about

12,000 prisoners. Moscow's Butyrka Prison squeezed 140 men into a cell designed to hold 24.

The Great Terror eventually ended. When his purpose was accomplished, Stalin then purged Yezhov, the top purger, and replaced him with Lavrenti Beria. Yezhov was not executed but given a token position and soon disappeared. Beria then argued that NKVD fascists had been responsible for the terror, and like Yezhov before him, he ordered the executions of nearly all senior NKVD officers and sent most of the others to the camps (many camp inmates briefly enjoyed seeing their former interrogators and torturers joining them).

Executions during the Great Terror were not limited to those purged; there still was an absolute requirement to liquidate "enemies of the people," party members with insufficient revolutionary consciousness, independent thinkers, and the like. Of those arrested, the number of the executed will never be known with certainty. The result of the Great Terror was a whole new Communist Party. Of 139 candidates and members of the party's central committee, 98 were shot. Only 59 of 1,966 delegates to the party congress in 1934 were alive to attend the 1939 congress. In total, the purge eliminated 850,000 members from the party, or 36 percent of the membership. Throughout the country, extravagant adulation of Stalin became common, while the population learned silence and obedience, fear and submission. It was a revolution not in structure but in personnel. Virtually all the old guard and the party faithful who had lived through the Russian Revolution were murdered.

Stalin had liquidated the old party; the new party was totally terrorized into obeying his slightest whim or command.

His power was absolute. He needed to obey no laws, no customs, no traditions. He feared no man under him. With no competing vision, he was free to seek out his own version of utopia, unhindered by any norms, traditions, or ethics.

How many were killed during this reign of terror? The published figure of 1,000,000 executed does not cover camp and transit deaths. In 1936, the camp population was largely generated by the collectivization campaign. When these camp deaths are included, along with an estimated 65,000 dying from deportation, and with the number shot, the total murdered in the years of the Great Terror is probably 4,345,000. This is a prudent estimate. Stalin's democide could be as high as 10,821,000 or as low as 2,044,000.

Overall, from 1928 until his death in 1953, Stalin murdered about 42,672,000 Russians, Poles, Hungarians, Bulgarians, Rumanians, Germans, Latvians, Lithuanians, Estonians, and Finns—more than twice the 20,946,000 whom Hitler murdered. Yet Mao would outdo both.

MAO'S CULTURAL REVOLUTION

The Great Famine that Mao purposely imposed from the late 1950s to the early 1960s described in chapter 6 helped to split the Chinese Communist Party. Many communists militantly and fervently supported Mao's desire to continue his Glorious Revolution. Opposed to him were powerful pragmatists, the "capitalist roaders," who wished to liberalize the economy and had forced him to end the "Great Leap Forward," the commune system of peasant factories, and the Great Famine. Mao wanted to purge his party much as

Stalin had done earlier in the Soviet Union. But when Mao began the purge, he instead created one of the most violent civil wars of the last century.

The purge began in May 1966, when he launched a public written attack on P'en Chen, mayor of Beijing and a member of the politburo. The chairman cast it in the form of a circular of the central committee and disseminated it throughout the party and the army. It was a call for war on the "the reactionary bourgeois stand of those so-called 'academic authorities' who oppose the Party and socialism," "the reactionary bourgeois ideas in the sphere of academic work, education, journalism, literature and art, and publishing," and "those representatives of the bourgeoisie who have sneaked into the Party, the government, the army, and all spheres of culture."

Mao's purpose in organizing and exciting the Cultural Revolution, therefore, was to discredit and overthrow his party opponents (the "capitalist roaders"), indoctrinate a whole new generation of proletarian revolutionaries, and create an ideological revolution among the masses—to replace old ideas with Mao's thought. It was to be the communist revolution all over again.

Mao went outside the party and appealed to the greatest source of brainwashed energy in the country—the students—who had been taught to adore and love Mao, the "Great helmsmen of China." He used the army to promote, direct, and support the idealism and energy of millions of high school and college students as he excited their rebellion against those who were now treated as enemies of the chairman. Massive meetings were held, involving millions of "Red Guards," as the students soon became known. They were encouraged to uncover "capitalist roaders" or "counterrevolutionaries" in every organization and then attack, torture, and murder such suspects in and out of the party.

Throughout August and September 1966, Red Guards conducted a reign of terror. People thought to be bourgeois or counterrevolutionaries were beaten in their homes and on the street; houses were invaded at will and ransacked; belongings that Red Guards viewed as unnecessary for a proletarian family were destroyed or confiscated. Possessing Western books, records, or goods was sufficient cause to be accused of spying. And as Premier Chou En-lai later admitted, "The police and soldiers were under orders not to interfere."

Even Central Committee members, mayors, and other prestigious officials were not exempt. The China News Agency admitted that there "was a special prison [apparently Qin Ching] outside of Peking where thirty-four senior leaders were tortured to death, twenty maimed, and sixty went insane during the Cultural Revolution." It secretly held at one time about five hundred of China's leaders, each isolated in a small cell, forbidden to talk to anyone, and known to their guards only by number. No word was allowed out about their imprisonment, even to their families.

Soon this revolution deteriorated into the murder of anyone who disagreed with how one faction or another defined Mao's thought or policies. Red Guard fought Red Guard, "leftist" military units fought "leftist" military units, and "conservative" workers and peasants fought both. In 1967, serious clashes and in some places heavy fighting broke out in all of China's twenty-six provinces and autonomous regions. In Szechwan, possibly in consequence of a split within the armed forces stationed in the province, heavy fighting was waged in which even gunboats, tanks, and artillery were involved.

Parts of cities and whole towns and villages were destroyed. In Wuhan in July 1967, an army unit mutinied, occupied key points, and led an "anti-left" uprising. In the wake of this, struggles broke out in Canton, spread to other parts of the military region, and were fought with great violence. One large wall poster put up in Canton in 1974 claimed that in "Guangdong Province alone nearly 40,000 revolutionary masses and cadres were massacred and more than 1,000,000 were imprisoned, put under 'control' and struggled against."

In 1968, there were "very serious" engagements, with army units involved on both sides of the battling factions. The deputy commander of the Wuhan Military Region declared that "the ammunition they had fired within the preceding several days would have sufficed 'to fight several battles in the war against Japan.'" Tens of thousands of militia troops surrounded Wuzhou and succeeded in taking the city after three weeks. Both sides suffered untold casualties; some areas were razed to the ground. The "Allied Command" took up to a thousand prisoners among the "April 22" faction, whom they treated cruelly. They would randomly pick out prisoners on forced marches to shoot on the spot. Family members, including the children of prisoners, were mercilessly slaughtered. The brutality matched the Japanese massacre in Nanjing. Liuzhou and Guilin were subject to similar holocausts, except that the latter, being the stronghold of "April 22" power, never fell to the "Allied Command."

In the countryside and the major cities of Kwangsi Province, violent battles went on for weeks and even involved tanks, artillery, and antiaircraft guns. Large urban areas were destroyed, and "gas shells or explosives were used to flush out those who were fighting from sewer ducts." This also happened in other provinces. In the cities of Suchou and Liuchou there were more than fifty thousand battle dead from military-like clashes between Red Guards and the army.

The violence against individuals by one fanatical faction or another continued everywhere. Incarceration, torture, and death were readily meted out to supposedly rich peasants, landlords, counterrevolutionaries, rightists, leftists, spies, or alleged sympathizers of opposing factions. Aside from party leaders and the usual bourgeoisie suspects, intellectuals, scientists, the educated, and the talented were also victims. At least in the Soviet Union under Stalin's bloody fist, science, learning, and expertise were not attacked per se. But as in Cambodia under the murderous Khmer Rouge, those Chinese intellectuals "who survived or escaped physical torment, were, at best, forced into a state of intellectual suspension or paralysis."

During the Cultural Revolution in China, the party was being destroyed at the center, and the very authority and power of communist rule was endangered. By 1969, seven out of seventeen members of the Politburo were expelled and declared to be enemies of the party; also purged were fifty-three of ninety-seven members of the Communist Party's Central Committee, four out of six regional first party secretaries, and twenty-three out of twenty-nine provincial first party secretaries. In the country as a whole, claimed Party General Secretary Hu Yaobang, from 1957 to the end of the Cultural Revolution, one hundred million people were persecuted, politically harassed, or victimized.

But Mao had won the battle. Opposing party leaders had been destroyed or shaken out of power. Having destroyed the "right," he could now move on the "left," which was out of control in many areas. He called upon loyal army units to restore order. The country was gradually brought under control at the cost of much greater military involvement and dictation in party affairs and decisions.

Scholars agree that the revolution ended in April 1969 with the Ninth Party Congress. While scattered bloody clashes and local anarchy were soon eliminated, reconstruction of the party, cleansing of residual party "rightists" and "leftists," and dampening the violent, chanting enthusiasm of Red Guard factions preoccupied Mao until his death in 1976. About seventeen million youths were sent to the countryside after 1967 to be disciplined, and by about 1975, it was conservatively estimated that seventy million educated youth had been deported to labor in the countryside and border regions. Moreover, executions continued apace. Those who were assigned to work in the countryside and then returned to the city without permission were executed; as were those who helped refugees to escape the country.

This was a pyrrhic victory, for Mao ultimately failed. After his death, in a "right-wing" coup, the "Gang of Four"—which included Mao's wife who managed the Cultural Revolution for Mao—were arrested and imprisoned. Deng Xiaoping, the "capitalist roader" who had been maltreated and dragged from power by the Red Guards, eventually took over the party and country. During the following years, economic and social pragmatism and liberalization—the line that Mao fought against so bloodily—was pursued and institutionalized. And Mao's "revolutionary masses" hardly remained so after his death, if they existed at all. Indeed, judging from the massive Beijing Tiananmen Square demonstrations in 1976 and especially in 1989, rather than becoming infused with communist revolutionary spirit, the masses increasingly demanded bourgeois democracy.

What was the human cost of the Cultural Revolution? Estimates vary widely. On the high side, estimates exceed 10,000,000 killed. One estimate of more than 18,000,000 dead is based on sources collected by the Republic of China. A communist "restricted internal publication" reported an estimate of 20,000,000 unnatural deaths during those years. Still another estimate claims 15,000,000 were killed. In evaluating these and many other estimates, it is most likely that both sides in the revolution murdered about 7,731,000, including those who died from mistreatment and malnutrition in prisons and concentration camps, "leftists" and "rightists," "counterrevolutionaries," "bourgeoisie," "spies," party officials and cadres, government officials and workers, more successful peasants, scientists, writers, teachers, students, those unlucky enough to be around—and, of course, husbands, wives, and even children who were murdered alongside their convicted family members. In addition, nearly 563,000 army troops, members of Red Guard factions, and rebelling peasants may have died in battle. And the revolution also aggravated a famine that killed around 1,000,000 people.

Add it all together, this revolution cost about 9,292,000 lives, which is greater than the total cost in lives of World

War I. All in one nation. And all to determine one thing: which thug's policies would rule.

• • •

Few would deny any longer what the previous bloody examples attest: communism—Marxism-Leninism and its variants—leads to bloody terrorism, deadly purges, lethal prison camps and forced labor, fatal deportations, man-made famines, extrajudicial executions and show trials, outright mass murder, and genocide. In total, communist (Marxist-Leninist) regimes murdered nearly 148 million people from 1917 to 1987. For a perspective on this incredible toll, note that all domestic and foreign wars during the twentieth century killed in combat around 41 million.

Communists, when in control of a nation, have murdered more than 3.6 times the number of people killed in combat in all wars, including the two world wars.

And what did communism, this greatest of human social experiments, achieve for its poor citizens at this most bloody cost in lives? Nothing. It left in its wake an economic, environmental, social, and cultural disaster.

The Khmer Rouge example provides insight into why communists believed it necessary and moral to massacre so many of their fellow humans. Their absolutist ideology was married to absolute power. They believed without a shred of doubt that they knew the truth, that they would bring about the greatest human welfare and happiness, and that to realize this utopia, they had to mercilessly tear down the old feudal or capitalist order and culture and then erect a totally new communist society.

The communists saw the construction of their utopia as a war on poverty, exploitation, imperialism, and inequality. And as in a real war, noncombatants were unfortunately caught in the battle, and then there were the necessary enemy casualties: the clergy, bourgeoisie, capitalists, "wreckers," intellectuals, counterrevolutionaries, rightists, tyrants, the rich, and landlords. In a war, millions may die, but these deaths may well be justified by the end, as in the defeat of Hitler in World War II. To many communists, the goal of a communist utopia was enough to justify all the deaths.

The irony of this is that communism in practice, even after decades of total control, did not improve the lot of the average person and, instead, usually made living conditions worse than before the revolution. Understandably, around thirty-five million people fled or escaped communist countries as refugees. This was an unequaled vote against communist utopian pretensions. Its equivalent would be everyone fleeing California, emptying it of all human life.

There is a supremely important lesson for human life and welfare to be learned from this horrendous sacrifice to one ideology:

> No one can be trusted with unlimited power. The more power a government has to impose the beliefs of an ideological or religious elite or decree the whims of a dictator, the more likely human lives and welfare will be sacrificed.

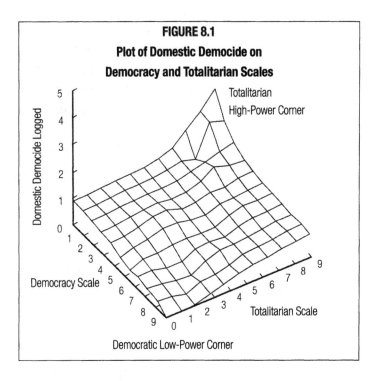

FIGURE 8.1

Plot of Domestic Democide on Democracy and Totalitarian Scales

Certainly, communism does not stand alone in such megamurders. We have the example of totalitarian-socialist Nazi Germany, the fascist Nationalist government of China under Chiang Kai-shek, the fascist Japanese militarists, and in recent years, the socialist thug of Iraq, Saddam Hussein, among others.

What connects all these cases of democide is this: as a government's power is more unrestrained, as its power reaches into all corners of culture and society, the more likely it is to kill its own citizens. As a governing elite has the power to do whatever it wants, whether to satisfy its most personal wishes, or to pursue what it believes is right and true, it may do so whatever the cost in lives. Here, power is the necessary condition for mass murder. Once an elite has full authority, other causes and conditions can operate to bring about the immediate genocide, terrorism, massacres, or whatever killing the members of an elite feel is warranted.

All this provides a solid, life oriented argument for democratic freedom:

Freedom preserves and secures life.

See, for example, Figure 8.1 on page 101.

That which preserves and protects human life is a moral good. And freedom is already a moral good because it promotes human welfare and minimizes internal political violence. Now, add to this list the moral good of saving human lives from war.

9

ON FREEDOM'S MORAL GOODS: ELIMINATING WAR

ALTHOUGH IT IS SOMETIMES the lesser evil, as in the war against Hitler, Saddam Hussein's Iraq, or the Taliban's Afghanistan, war is always a horror. It consumes human lives and property with a most savage appetite. Humanists, idealists, and pacifists have focused on war as the supreme human problem that mankind must solve. Stacks of books provide histories of war, analyses of its causes and conditions, and solutions. Now, finally, a well-researched, well-studied solution is at hand. It is practical. It is much desired for itself. It is consistent with human rights. It is supported by clear theory.

To introduce this solution, I need not describe what happens in war to human bodies and souls. Through documentaries, movies, television, and books on war, we are doubtlessly familiar with all its horrors. But what is not widely known is that dictators of all kinds have murdered several times more people than has combat in all the wars, foreign and domestic. As horrible as it was, the Hutu rulers of Rwanda killed more people in four months than did the 1916 battle of the Somme, considered one of the deadliest battles of all time, during the same length of time. And this was only one murderous government in a fairly small country. Virtually all proposals to prevent war have suffered from this defect: they ignore how dictators and dictatorships differ from democratic leaders and democracies.

There have always been those who, when they inherit or seize power, forcefully fill the ranks of their army with unwilling soldiers and then grind them to death in a war to grab more power and control over others. The rogues' gallery of these megamurderers and aggressors is long, and surely at the top would be, for the twentieth century alone, Hitler, Stalin, Lenin, Mao, Chiang Kai-shek, Tojo Hideki, and Pol Pot. When there are such people controlling large armies, the solutions to war—such as pacifism, unilateral disarmament, or disarmament treaties—do not work. Worse, these solutions weaken or disarm democracies and make the world safe only for tyrants and dictators and thugs.

Now, finally, we have the proven knowledge to avoid both wars and the aggression of dictators. This solution was proposed in the latter part of the eighteenth century, and recent social science research has shown its veracity. In his *Perpetual Peace,* written in 1795, the German philosopher Immanuel Kant argued that the way to universal peace lay in creating republics, or what today we would call representative democracies.

Note two things about this solution. First is that, where people have equal rights and freely participate in their governance, people will be unlikely to promote a war in which they or their loved ones might die and their property be destroyed. And second, where leaders are responsible to their people as voters, leaders will be unwilling to resort to fighting wars. When both leaders of two nations are so restrained, war between them should not occur.

Full proof of this claim had to wait, however, until social scientists could develop research methods to document it. Thanks in part to the growth of new statistical models made possible by the advent of computers, in the 1980s and 1990s quantitative researchers proved Kant to be correct. By then they had collected data on all wars that had occurred over the last several centuries, and by applying various statistical analyses to these data, they established that there never (or virtually never) has been a war between well-established democracies.

Moreover, through these techniques, social scientists also proved that there was no hidden factor accounting for this,

TABLE 9.1
International Wars, 1816–2005

Belligerents	Wars*
Democracies vs. Democracies	0
Democracies vs. Nondemocracies	166
Nondemocracies vs. Nondemocracies	205

*At least 1,000 killed

Incidents of International Violence of Any Kind, 1973–2005

Belligerents	Violent Incidents[†]
Democracies vs. Democracies	0
Democracies vs. Nondemocracies	18
Nondemocracies vs. Nondemocracies	42

[†]At least 1 killed

SOURCES: Melvin, Small, and J. Davis Singer, SIPRI, PRIO, Monty Marshall, R. J. Rummel

such as a lack of common borders or geographic distance between democracies. Nor was this democratic peace attributable to the wealth of democracies or their international power, education levels, technology, resources, religion, or population density. The findings are straightforward:

> Well-established democracies do not
> make war on each other.

On this, see Table 9.1 on page 105.

WARS FROM 1816 TO 2005 AND INCIDENTS OF VIOLENCE

As shown in the table, for all 371 pairs of nations involved in wars against each other from 1816 to 2005, not one pair was a democracy making war on another democracy. Moreover, of sixty incidents of violence less than war between nations from 1973 to 2005, not one was between two democratic countries. And finally, there are now 122 democracies among the 192 nations of the world today, but there is no war or violence between any of them; they do not consider each other a threat to their security, and they do not arm against each other. The long unprotected border between Canada and the United States is the norm among democracies.

Is this lack of war and violence by chance? good luck? We can calculate the likelihood that democracies have not gone to war or committed violence against each other. Different researchers have tested the lack of war and violence for different years, different definitions of democracy, and different ways of defining war. And in those studies using tests of statistical significance, the positive result has been statistically significant in each case. Thus, the overall significance of this absence of war and violence is really a multiple (or function, since some of these studies using the same data are not statistically independent) of these different significant tests, which would make the overall probability (subjectively estimated) of the results occurring by chance alone surely millions to one.

• • •

There is a near perfect correlation between the lack of freedom in two nations and the number of people killed in wars between them.

It is not just a free, democratic populace that inhibits war, but also the *degree* to which people are free. To understand this, we must stop thinking about war as a single event that happens or does not happen. Rather, we should think of war as embodying different amounts of killing. A war may be as vast in scope as World War I or World War II in which the fighting between Germany and the Soviet Union alone took more than 7,500,000 lives. But the severity of a war may only be in hundreds killed, not millions—as was the war between India and China in 1962, at a cost to each of around 500 dead, or the Gulf War, when the United States lost 148 people from battle and 35 from friendly fire. All are wars, but the relevant distinction among them here is one of magnitude.

Imagine a yardstick of freedom, with democracies like Canada, New Zealand, and Sweden at one end, and the least free countries like North Korea, Sudan, Burma, Cuba, and Laos at the other. Toward the middle would be such authoritarian countries as Egypt, Bangladesh, and Malaysia. Then, for any two countries, the closer the government of each is to the democratic end of the yardstick, the more likely it is that there will be fewer killed in any war between them. Thus we can establish a correlation between the degree of freedom and the degree of intensity in war.

To the iron law that democracies do not make war on each other, we can now add:

> The less democratically free any two nations are, the more likely is severe violence between them.

There are many other kinds of international violence besides war. There is violence short of war, such as American aircraft shooting down Iraqi fighters that violated the U.N.-defined no-fly zone over southern Iraq in the late 1990s, the blowing up of a South Korean passenger plane by North Korean agents, or military action by Cuban forces against Somalia during the Ethiopia-Somalia War over the Ogaden (1976–83). And despite this absence of violence *between* democracies, democracies overall can be violent and aggressive.

> Democracies direct violence only at non-democracies.

However, when one considers the explanation for why democracies are peaceful—that democratic peoples are acculturated into negotiation and compromise over violence—one should expect that democracies overall would have the least severe foreign violence and war, the least dead in all their violence in fighting with other countries. Another way of putting this would be, the more freedom a nation has, the less its leaders squander the lives of their people in foreign violence and war.

> The less democratic a country is,
> the more intense its foreign violence.

This is not to say that democracies are generally pacifist. They have engaged in bloody wars, usually to fight aggression and defend themselves and other democracies. And certainly democracies have also been the aggressors, as was the United States in the Spanish-American War, the Philippine-American War of 1899–1902, the Grenada and Panama interventions, and the Afghanistan and Iraq invasions. On the average, however, democratic leaders are more careful with the lives of their citizens, and therefore, they fight less severe wars.

There also are exceptions to this, as in the battle of the Somme during which the British generals continued to throw their troops into battle even after suffering bloody losses and lack of success. However, the horror of this for British public opinion was so great as to make British foreign policy naively pacifist for the next generation. Totalitarian regimes have no such negative feedback. Their dictators can, time after time, in war after war, use their people as mass instruments of war, like bullets and shells, throwing them at the enemy in human waves for whatever purpose.

As a species, we have been killing ourselves by the millions in war after war throughout history. Now, finally, we have the power of knowledge to end forever—or at the very least drastically reduce—all this human slaughter. Freedom gives us the answer.

We must foster democratic freedom for all humanity to end this bloody scourge.

Until all people everywhere enjoy this freedom, we must foster at least some freedom where none exists in order to lessen the mass killing incumbent with the prosecution of wars. War is an evil, and the fact that free people have fought wars in order to preserve their freedom makes it no less so. What would eliminate this evil must be a moral good.

> Therefore, lessening and potentially ending war is another moral good of freedom.

Why is it that free and democratic peoples do not make war on each other? This peacekeeping factor is analogous to what inhibits democratic nations from internal political violence, as described in chapter 7. Where democratic freedom flourishes in two countries, where there are free markets and freedom of religion, association, ideas, and speech, then societies of mutual interest—such as corporations, partnerships, associations, societies, churches, schools, and clubs—proliferate in and between countries. Examples of these are the Red Cross, the Association of Tennis Professionals, and the International Studies Association. These cross-national groups become separate pyramids of power, competing with each other and with governments. As a result, both democratic nations then are sewn together into one society, one crosscut by these multifold groups, with multiple bonds between them.

Moreover, between democratic governments there are many official and unofficial connections and linkages that achieve similar functions and satisfy mutual interests. Their militaries freely coordinate strategies and may even share equipment in line with their mutual defense arrangements and perceived common dangers. An example of this would be nuclear weapons and military equipment shared by Great Britain and the United States. Intelligence services will share some secrets and even sometimes agents. Health services will coordinate their studies, undertake common projects, and provide health supplies when needed. Such multiple shared interests bond these governments together.

Politicians, leaders, and groups, therefore, have a common interest in keeping the peace. And where conflict might escalate into violence, such as over trade issues or fishing rights, interests are so cross-pressured by different groups and ties that the depth of feeling and single-minded devotion to the interest at stake is simply not there. Keep in mind that for democratic leaders to choose to make the huge jump to war against another country, there must be almost fanatical dedication to the interests—the stakes—involved, almost to the exclusion of all else.

There is also something about democracies that is even more important than these links, bonds, and cross-pressures. This is their democratic culture. Democratic peoples see one another as willing to compromise and negotiate issues rather than fighting violently over them. More important, they see one another as the same kind—part of one's in-group, one's moral universe. They each share not only socially, in overlapping groups, functions, and linkages, but also in political culture. Americans and Canadians, for example, have no expectation of fighting each other over trade restrictions and disputes. Both see each other as similarly free, democratic, and willing to bargain. And therefore, they have a totally unarmed 5,525-mile border between them. Similarly, with the development of a solid liberal democracy in Japan since the end of World War II, there is now no expectation of war between Japan and any other democracy, including the United States and democratic South Korea.

Finally, credit should be given to the ideology of democratic liberalism itself. Philosophical (or classical) democratic liberals believe in the right of people to make their voices heard, to have a role in government, and to be free. Such liberals—who in domestic policy may be conservative, progressive, social democrat, Democrat, or Republican—greatly oppose any violence against other democracies. Even if those in power should consider such actions, democratic liberals—who compose the vast majority of intellectuals, journalists, and politicians—would arouse a storm of protest against them.

To summarize, there is no war between democracies because their people are free. This freedom creates a multitude of groups that produce diverse linkages across borders and cross-pressured interests and make for an exchange culture of negotiation and compromise. A free people sees another free people as being of the same kind, as morally similar, as negotiators instead of aggressors, and therefore they have no expectation of war; there is a prevalent ideology of democratic liberalism that believes in democratic freedom and opposes violence between democracies.

Then why do dictators make war on each other? Do not dictators see each other as being of the same kind, sharing the same coercive culture? Yes, and that is exactly the problem for them. They live by coercion and force. Their guns keep them in power. They depend on a controlled populace manipulated by propaganda, deceit, and fear. Commands and decrees are the working routine of dictators; negotiations are a battleground in which one wins through lies, subterfuge, misinformation, stalling, and manipulation.

Dictators' international relations are no different. They see them as war fought by other means. They will only truly negotiate in the face of bigger and better guns, and they will only keep their promises as long as those guns remain pointed at them. This is also how one dictator sees another—and incidentally, how they see democracies. This is not to say that war necessarily will happen between two countries if one or both is not democratic. They may be too far away from each other, too weak, or too inhibited by the greater power of a third country. It is only to say that the governments of such countries lack the social and cultural inhibitions that would prevent armed conflict between them, that their dictatorial governments inherently encourage war. War may not happen, but it can, and the more undemocratic the governments, the more likely it will.

CONCLUSION

THE POWER OF FREEDOM to end war, minimize violence within nations, and eradicate genocide and mass murder seems almost magical. It is as though we have a single-drug cure for cancer. Had I not actually done much of the research myself over more than forty years, I would have doubted this. Yet my work and that of other social scientists and scholars has proven it true. See, for example, Table 10.1 on page 116.

Our knowledge of the peace-creating and peacemaking effects of freedom now gives us a nonviolent way to promote a nonviolent world. As should now be clear:

Democratic freedom is a method of nonviolence.

Enhancing, spreading, and promoting human rights and democracy are the way to enhance, spread, and promote nonviolence. Proponents of nonviolence have worked out many peaceful tactics for opposing dictators,

TABLE 10.1

Deaths by Cause and Freedom Rating (in Millions), 1900–1987

	Free	Partly Free	Unfree	Totals
Famine	0	14	>60	>75
Democide*	0	26	103	129
International War†	2	19	34	55
Civil War‡	0	5	6	11
Total	3	65	>203	>271

*Domestic genocide and mass murder. SOURCE: R. J. Rummel, *Statistics of Democide*. Includes nation-state and quasi-state regimes.

† Includes combat dead and other civilian war dead. Excludes wartime democide. From diverse sources, including that for democide.

‡ For 141 state-level regimes. Excludes democide. Source same as for democide above.

such as sit-down strikes, general strikes, mass demonstrations, refusal to pay taxes, underground newspapers, sabotage by excessive obedience to the rules, and the like. Much thought has gone into how a people can nonviolently promote human rights. Overall, however, nonviolence works best among a free people:

> Freedom itself promotes a nonviolent solution to
> social problems and conflicts.

In conclusion, we have wondrous human freedom as a moral force for the good. Freedom produces social justice, creates wealth and prosperity, minimizes violence, saves human lives, and is a solution to war. In two words, it creates human security. Moreover, and most important,

> People should not be free only because it is
> good for them. They should be free because
> it is their right as human beings.

In opposition to freedom is power, its antagonist. While freedom is a right, the power to govern is a privilege granted by a people to those they elect and hold responsible for its use. Too often, however, thugs seize control of a people by force and use their weaponry to make their power total and absolute. Where freedom produces wealth and prosperity, such absolute power causes impoverishment and famine. Where freedom minimizes internal violence, eliminates genocide and mass murder, and solves the problem of war, such absolute power unleashes internal violence, murders millions, and produces the bloodiest wars. In short,

Power kills, and absolute power kills absolutely.

Now, to summarize this book, why freedom?

Freedom is every person's right. And it is a moral good in that it promotes wealth, prosperity, social justice, and nonviolence, and it preserves human life.

AFTERWORD

I HAVE USED NOTES to document some of the facts I assert here and have provided bibliographies for work on democide and the democratic peace. However, those who want more documentation and supporting theory, analyses, and data, should visit my Web site at www.hawaii.edu/powerkills. There, I have documented all the facts and assertions that I have made here. The Web site includes my related books, some published articles, and papers with the relevant footnotes, documentation, and references one might desire. The list of these is at www.hawaii.edu/powerkills/list.htm. I also maintain a topical archive of posts on my democratic peace blog at www.hawaii.edu/powerkills/z.blog.archive .htm, many of which are relevant to what has been presented here.

NOTES

CHAPTER 1: OVERVIEW

p. 11: 272,000,000: This is a midestimate of the democide (genocide, massacres, atrocities, assassinations, extrajudicial executions, and other murder by government) during the last century, most by Marxist regimes. The estimates, sources, calculations, and notes are contained in Rummel, *Statistics of Democide*, and are published in full at www .hawaii.edu/powerkills/note5.htm.

Among all the democide estimates appearing in this book, some have been revised upward since their previous publication. I have changed that for Mao's 1958–62 famine from zero to 38,000,000. And thus I have had to change the overall democide for the People's Republic of China (1928–87) from 38,702,000 to 76,702,000. See freedoms-peace.blogspot.com/2005/11/reevaluating-chinas-democide -to-be.html.

I have changed my estimate for colonial democide from 870,000 to an additional 50,000,000. See freedomspeace .blogspot.com/2005/12/reevaluating-colonial-democide.html.

Thus, the new world total: old total (1900–1999) = 174,000,000 + 38,000,000 (new for China) + 50,000,000 (new for colonies) = 262,000,000. Just to give perspective on the incredible scale of this murder by government, if all the bodies were laid head to toe, with the average height being five feet, they would circle the earth ten times. Also, this democide murdered six times more people than died in combat in all the foreign and internal wars of the century. Finally, given popular estimates of the dead in a major nuclear war, this total democide is as though such a war did occur, but with the killing spread over a century.

p. 12: Human rights: See, P. R. Ghandhi, ed., *Blackstone's International Human Rights Documents* (London: Blackstone Press, 2000); and E. Lawson, comp., *Encyclopedia of Human Rights*, 2nd ed. (London: Taylor & Francis, 1996).

p. 16: Well established: The fact that democracies do not go to war against each other and that more than two hundred million people have been murdered by governments may be incredible. Therefore I have included two bibliographies, one on the sources of information and data on government democide, and the other on the peacefulness of democracies (called the democratic peace).

CHAPTER 2: THE RIGHTS OF ALL PEOPLE

p. 17: Want to be free: This is not a matter of speculation but has been clearly shown by international surveys. See, e.g., the publications of the World Values Survey at www.worldvaluessurvey.org.

p. 20: International law: The international legal basis for human rights is the International Bill of Human Rights passed in 1948 by the U.N. General Assembly. Its annex contains the Universal Declaration of Human Rights; International Covenant on Economic, Social and Cultural Rights;

International Covenant on Civil and Political Rights; Optional Protocol to the International Covenant on Civil and Political Rights; and the Second Optional Protocol to the International Covenant on Civil and Political Rights, aiming at the abolition of the death penalty. Note that these rights are not optional. In 1999, the General Assembly passed the Declaration on the Right and Responsibility of Individuals, Groups and Organs of Society to Promote and Protect Universally Recognized Human Rights and Fundamental Freedoms. See M. Glen Johnson and Janusz Symonides, *The Universal Declaration of Human Rights: A History of Its Creation and Implementation, 1948–1998* (Paris: UNESCO, 1998).

CHAPTER 3: THE JUSTNESS OF FREEDOM

p. 21: A social contract: My view of the social contract is close to that of John Rawls, *A Theory of Justice*, rev. ed. (Cambridge, MA: Harvard University Press, 1971).

p. 23: Legal government, sovereign and independent: This actually requires that other governments recognize that this government exists and has effective control and authority over the country. This usually involves the establishment of diplomatic relations.

p. 23: Self-determination: See Karen Knop, *Diversity and Self-Determination in International Law* (New York: Cambridge University Press, 2005); and Hurst Hannum, *Autonomy, Sovereignty, and Self-Determination: The Accommodation of Conflicting Rights* (Philadelphia: University of Pennsylvania Press, 1996).

p. 24: Right to immigrate: See Leonore Loeb Adler and Uwe P. Gielen, eds., *Migration: Immigration and Emigration in International Perspective* (Westport, CT: Praeger, 2003).

CHAPTER 4: THE INSTITUTIONS OF DEMOCRACY

p. 25: A democracy necessarily involves: Democracy cannot be looked at alone to understand it, but it must be compared to its competing political systems. Of the many works on this, I have found S. E. Finer, *Comparative Government* (New York: Basic Books, 1971), most helpful while still pertinent to contemporary regimes. My discrimination of political characteristics reflects his typology and survey, without following it in detail. Moreover, in my view, one cannot well divide these characteristics into different regime types without careful attention to the underlying political ideologies. On them, see Noel O'Sullivan, ed., *The Structure of Modern Ideology: Critical Perspectives on Social and Political Theory* (Brookfield, VT: Gower, 1989); Kenneth R. Minogue, *Alien Powers: The Pure Theory of Ideology* (New York: St. Martin's Press, 1985); and, in particular, William Ebenstein and Edwin Fogelman, *Today's Isms: Communism, Fascism, Capitalism, Socialism*, 9th ed. (Englewood Cliffs, NJ: Prentice-Hall, 1985).

p. 27: Of the 192 nations: The following statistics are from Freedom House. See *Freedom in the World 2006: The Annual Survey of Political Rights and Civil Liberties*, rev. ed. (Lanham, MD: Rowman & Littlefield, 2006). The Freedom House criteria by which its area experts judge the degree of freedom in a country are comparative, comprehensive, and explicit. See www.freedomhouse.org.

p. 27: Impeachment and trial of William Jefferson Clinton: I am not interested in defending or condemning Clinton, but rather in providing a nonpartisan account that illustrates how democracy operates to resolve peacefully the most important conflicts. See Daniel Cohen, *The Impeachment of William Jeffer-*

son Clinton (Brookfield, CT: Twenty-First Century Books, 1999); and Richard A. Posner, *An Affair of State: The Investigation, Impeachment, and Trial of President Clinton*, rev. ed. (Cambridge, MA: Harvard University Press, 2000).

p. 35: Year 2000 American presidential election: See Richard A. Posner, *Breaking the Deadlock: The 2000 Election, the Constitution, and the Courts* (Princeton, NJ: Princeton University Press, 2001).

CHAPTER 5: FREEDOM'S MORAL GOODS: WEALTH AND PROSPERITY

p. 38: Unbeatable engine of technological and economic growth: On the role of freedom, see Robert J. Barro, *Determinants of Economic Growth: A Cross-Country Empirical Study* (Cambridge, MA: MIT Press, 1997); Amartya Sen, *Development as Freedom* (New York: Oxford University Press, 2001); and Morton H. Halperin, Joseph T. Siegle, and Michael M. Weinstein, *The Democracy Advantage: How Democracies Promote Prosperity and Peace* (New York: Routledge, 2005).

p. 39: Consider the life of William "Bill" Gates: See James Wallace and Jim Erickson, *Hard Drive: Bill Gates and the Making of the Microsoft Empire* (New York: Harper Business, 1993), and Sara Barton-Wood, *Bill Gates: Computer Giant* (Austin: Raintree Steck-Vaughan, 2001).

p. 43: Lenin's Command Economy: For what the economy was like under the Soviets, see Vincent Barnett, *The Revolutionary Russian Economy, 1890–1940: Ideas, Debates and Alternatives* (New York: Routledge, 2004); James D. White, *Lenin: The Practice and Theory of Revolution* (New York: Palgrave Macmillan, 2001).

p. 48: Stalin's Command Economy: See Paul R. Gregory, ed., *Behind the Facade of Stalin's Command Economy: Evidence from the Soviet State and Party Archives* (Stanford, CA: Hoover Institution Press, 2001).

p. 51: Mao Tse-tung's Command Economy: See Leo Goodstadt, *China's Search for Plenty: The Economics of Mao Tse-tung* (New York: Weatherhill, 1973); and Hua-yu Li, *Mao and the Economic Stalinization of China, 1948–1953* (Lanham, MD: Rowman & Littlefield, 2006).

CHAPTER 6: FREEDOM'S MORAL GOODS: NO FAMINE EVER

p. 58: No democratically free people have ever had a famine: More than eighty-six million people died in famines in the twentieth century. Not one of them was in a democracy or occurred in India while it was a democracy. Consider the work of Amartya Sen, for example, the 1998 Nobel Prize winner in economics from India. At the age of twenty-three, he became the youngest chairman of the Department of Economics at Jadavpur University. He has been the president of the Econometric Society (1984), the International Economic Association (1986–89), the Indian Economic Association (1989), and the American Economic Association (1994). He is now master of Trinity College Cambridge. So he should know something about India. Sen says, as well, that no democracy has had a famine, and as far as India is concerned, its last famine was the 1943 Bengal famine, when India was a colony of Britain. See Sen, *Development as Freedom*, 180.

p. 58: The Great American Dust Bowl: See Tricia Andryszewski, *The Dust Bowl: Disaster on the Plains* (Brookfield, CT:

Millbrook Press, 1993); and Sean Price, *The Dirty Thirties: Documenting the Dust Bowl* (Chicago: Raintree, 2006).

p. 59: The Irish Famine: See Cathal Poirteir, ed., *The Great Irish Famine* (Chester Springs, PA: Dufour, 1999); and Susan Campbell Bartoletti, *Black Potatoes: The Story of the Great Irish Famine, 1845–1850* (Boston: Houghton Mifflin, 2005).

p. 60: Mao's Greatest Famine Ever: See Jasper Becker, *Hungry Ghosts: Mao's Secret Famine* (New York: Henry Holt, 1998); R. J. Rummel, *China's Bloody Century: Genocide and Mass Murder Since 1900* (New Brunswick, NJ: Transaction Publishers, 1991), chap. 11.

p. 61: Nearly 38 million people starved to death: From my research on China, I estimated that twenty-seven million Chinese starved to death or died from associated diseases in Mao's famine of 1958–62. Others estimated the toll to be as high as forty million. Jung Chang and Jon Halliday (*Mao: The Unknown Story* [New York: Anchor Books: 2006]) place the toll at thirty-eight million, and given their sources, I can accept that now.

CHAPTER 7: FREEDOM'S MORAL GOODS: MINIMIZING POLITICAL VIOLENCE

p. 63: This is a statistical fact: See R. J. Rummel, *Power Kills: Democracy as a Method of Nonviolence* (New Brunswick, NJ: Transaction Publishers, 1997), chap. 5.

p. 66: This "spontaneous society": For an elaboration of this theory of democratic freedom's inherent peacefulness, see Rummel, *Power Kills*, pt. 2. The fundamental idea is of a spontaneous society versus a coercive organization, or social field versus antifield.

p. 69: Lenin's Red Terror and Peasant War: See R. J. Rummel, *Lethal Politics: Soviet Genocide and Mass Murder Since 1917* (New Brunswick, NJ: Transaction Publishers, 1990), chap. 2; Sergey Petrovich Melgounov, *The Red Terror in Russia* (London: Dent & Sons, 1925); Mikhail Heller and Aleksandr Nekrich, *Utopia in Power: The History of the Soviet Union from 1917 to the Present*, trans. Phyllis B. Carlos (New York: Summit Books, 1986); and Robert Conquest, *V. I. Lenin* (New York: Viking Press, 1972).

CHAPTER 8: ON FREEDOM'S MORAL GOODS: ELIMINATING DEMOCIDE

p. 75: On Freedom's Moral Goods: Eliminating Democide: The incredible human toll from genocide and mass murder (democide) and its history is virtually unknown, even among scholars. So I have appended a related bibliography to this book.

p. 75: 272,000,000 men, women, and children: See the note above to chapter 1, p. 7.

p. 76 But there was also: For the following estimates, see Rummel, *Death by Government*, and Rummel, *Statistics of Democide*.

p. 77: Rwanda's Great Genocide: See Philip Gourevitch, *We Wish to Inform You That Tomorrow We Will Be Killed with Our Families: Stories from Rwanda* (New York: Picador, 1999); Scott Straus, *The Order of Genocide: Race, Power, and War in Rwanda* (Ithaca, NY: Cornell University Press, 2006); and Thomas P. Odom, *Journey into Darkness: Genocide in Rwanda* (College Station: Texas A&M University Press, 2005).

p. 80: Pol Pot's Killing Fields: For the historical context of this killing, see Rummel, *Death by Government*, chap. 9.

See also Ben Kiernan, *The Pol Pot Regime: Race, Power, and Genocide in Cambodia Under the Khmer Rouge, 1975–79* (New Haven, CT: Yale University Press, 2002).

p. 81: As many as 2.4 million: For the estimates, sources, and calculations of these killed, see Rummel, *Statistics of Democide*, chap. 4.

p. 86: Stalin's Great Terror: See Robert Conquest, *Great Terror*, rev. ed. (New York: Macmillan, 1973), and Robert Conquest, *The Great Terror: A Reassessment* (New York: Oxford University Press, 1991).

p. 92: Stalin murdered about 42,672,000: This estimate is based on the calculations in Rummel, *Lethal Politics*.

p. 92: Mao's Cultural Revolution: See R. J. Rummel, *China's Bloody Century: Genocide and Mass Murder Since 1900* (New Brunswick, NJ: Transaction Publishers, 1991), chap. 12; Chi-Tsai Feng and Feng Jicai, *Ten Years of Madness: Oral Histories of China's Cultural Revolution* (San Francisco: China Books and Periodicals; 1996); Joseph W. Esherick, Paul G. Pickowicz, and Andrew G. Walder, *China's Cultural Revolution as History* (Stanford, CA: Stanford University Press, 2006); and Simon Leys and Pierre Ryckmans, *The Chairman's New Clothes: Mao and the Cultural Revolution* (New York: Palgrave Macmillan, 1978).

p. 98: This revolution cost about 9,292,000 lives: This estimate is based on calculations in Rummel, *China's Bloody Century*.

p. 99: Murdered nearly 148 million people from 1917 to 1987: This count for Marxist regimes is based on Rummel, *Lethal Politics*; Rummel, *China's Bloody Century*; Rummel, *The Statistics of Democide*; and the updated estimates mentioned above in note to chapter 1, p. 7.

CHAPTER 9: ON FREEDOM'S MORAL GOODS: ELIMINATING WAR

p. 103: On Freedom's Moral Goods: Eliminating War: A well-researched, well-studied solution is at hand. This is called the democratic peace, the most important and well-researched idea in international relations and a pillar of American foreign policy under President Bill Clinton and a foundation of American foreign policy under President George W. Bush. Because of this importance, I have appended to this book an extensive bibliography on the democratic peace.

p. 105: Not one pair was a democracy making war on another democracy: Many exceptions to this proposition have been proposed, but not one stands up on analysis. The major exceptions claimed are the following, within the major reason for rejecting the claim in parenthesis:

- Athens vs. various democratic city-states, 427 BC–369 BC (no battles; other city-states are not perceived as a democracy by Athens; not autonomous; vague history)
- United States vs. Britain (1812) (Britain not a democracy)
- Georgia vs. Cherokee nation (1828) (Cherokees oligarchic and undemocratic)
- Zurich, Bern et al. vs. Lucerne (1847) (Lucerne a virtual dictatorship)
- France vs. Roman Republic (1849) (transient democracies, Roman Republic not an independent state)
- U.S. Civil War (1861) (Confederacy oligarchic, not an independent state; not seen as democratic)
- Chile vs. Peru (1879) (both oligarchic)
- France vs. Britain (1897) (bloodless Niger-Fashoda crisis)

- United States vs. Spain (1898) (Spain controlled by a monarchy)
- Britain vs. Boer Republics (1899) (Boer franchise limited to some whites)
- United States vs. Philippine Republic (1899) (new Philippine government oligarchic)
- United States and the Allies vs. Germany (1914) (German autocratic government in foreign and military policy)
- Britain vs. Finland (1941) (Finish autocrats took control and rejected democracy during the war; no Finn-British battles)
- Israel vs. Lebanon (1948) (Lebanon ruled by oligarchic elites)
- United States vs. Guatemala (1954) (Guatemala engaged in authoritarian repression, bloodless conflict for United States)
- Britain vs. Iceland (1972, 1975) (bloodless, only shots across fishing-boat bows)
- Peru vs. Ecuador (1981) (border clashes, both countries authoritarian)
- Britain vs. Argentina (Falkland Islands War, 1982) (Argentina a military dictatorship)
- Serbia vs. Slovenia (1991) (countries a year-old and verged on autocratic)
- Serbia vs. Croatia (1991) (countries a year-old and verged on autocratic)

ANNOTATED BIBLIOGRAPHY ON DEMOCIDE

GENERAL WORKS

These are sources providing general or comparative analyses that include totalitarian states or statistics on democide in more than one of them. Throughout the annotations, when the authors use *genocide* broadly to mean what I am calling *democide* (murder by government), I employ the latter term to describe their work.

Chalk, Frank, and Kurt Jonassohn. *The History and Sociology of Genocide: Analysis and Case Studies.* New Haven: Yale University Press, 1990. 461 pp. Published in cooperation with the Montreal Institute for Genocide Studies.

This is an important and seminal overview of democide throughout history. Through excerpts from major and often original works on genocide and mass murder, the authors also cover the most infamous cases of democide in the twentieth century. Most relevant here are their chapters on the Holocaust and Stalin's and Pol Pot's democides.

Charny, Israel W., ed. *Genocide: A Critical Bibliographic Review.* London: Mansell; New York: Facts on File, 1988. 273 pp.

Charny offers bibliographic chapters on the Holocaust, the Cambodian democide, and the Soviet genocidal famine in Ukraine.

Charny, Israel W., ed. *Genocide: A Critical Bibliographic Review,* vol. 2. London: Mansell; New York: Facts on File, 1991. 432 pp.

This second volume contains bibliographic chapters on the Holocaust and a number of general chapters relevant to democide by totalitarian states.

Charny, Israel W., ed. *Toward the Understanding and Prevention of Genocide: Proceedings of the International Conference on the Holocaust and Genocide.* Boulder, CO: Westview Press, 1984. 396 pp.

This collection of papers on genocide and mass murder is a ground-breaking contribution to our knowledge of such killing. In addition to chapters dealing with the Holocaust, these papers also cover the genocide by China in Tibet, the Cambodian democide, and the Soviet genocidal famine in Ukraine.

Glaser, Kurt, and Stefan T. Possony. *Victims of Politics: The State of Human Rights.* New York: Columbia University Press, 1979. 614 pp.

In considering human rights, the authors comprehensively deal with all aspects of mass murder, including the Holocaust and Soviet and Communist Chinese democide. Moreover, these are treated as relevant in chapters on torture, forced labor, genocide (see particularly the chronology of genocide, mass expulsions and forced migrations, and the oppression of nationalities). This is one of the most comprehensive works on human rights in all its meanings and a useful starting work for those beginning study in this area.

Horowitz, Irving Louis. *Taking Lives: Genocide and State Power.* 3rd ed. New Brunswick, NJ: Transaction Books, 1980. 199 pp.

In this revision of his *Genocide: State Power and Mass Murder* (1976), Horowitz argues for a new typology of societies that would take into account their mass killings of human beings. At one side of a scale he suggests would-be genocidal societies, at the other permissive societies. This is an innovative work and an ideal source for those doing conceptual-theoretical work on democide.

Kuper, Leo. *Genocide: Its Political Use in the Twentieth Century.* New Haven, CT: Yale University Press, 1981. 255 pp.

This is a must read for students of democide. Kuper offers overviews of state murder, while covering the historical and political context and the relevant international conventions. He presents a helpful overview of theories of democide and describes its social structure and process. His analysis of democide and the sovereign state is important for those who neglect the international legal framework that permits such mass murder.

Rummel, R. J. *Death by Government.* New Brunswick, NJ: Transactions Publishers, 1994. 496 pp.

This is Rummel's fourth book in a series devoted to comparative democide. He presents the primary results in tables and figures as well as a historical sketch of the major cases of democide, those in which one million or more people were killed by a regime. His results clearly and decisively show that democracies commit less democide than other regimes. The underlying principle is that the less freedom people have, the greater the violence; the more freedom, the less the violence. Thus, he says, "The problem is power. The solution is democracy. The course of action is to foster freedom."

Totten, Samuel, and William S. Parsons, eds. "Special Section: Teaching About Genocide." *Social Education* 55, no. 2 (1991): 84–133.

Totten and Parsons deal with the Nazi genocide of the Jews and Gypsies and the Cambodian and Soviet democides; presents a brief list of genocidal acts during this century (p. 129).

Veenhoven, Willem A., and Winifred Crum Ewing, eds. *Case Studies on Human Rights and Fundamental Freedoms: A World Survey.* 5 vols. The Hague: Nijhoff, 1975–76. Published for the Foundation for the Study of Plural Societies.

Includes chapters on Eastern Europe, Communist China, and the Soviet gulag. Some articles, such as the one on the gulag, provide specific information on democide.

Wallimann, Isidor, and Michael N. Dobkowski, eds. *Genocide and the Modern Age: Etiology and Case Studies of Mass Death.* New York: Greenwood Press, 1987. 322 pp.

Contains important taxonomic, theoretical, and overview chapters. The theoretical chapters on the Holocaust by John K. Roth, Alan Rosenberg, and Robert G. L. Waite are of particular relevance here.

CALCULATIONS OF OVERALL DEMOCIDE

Elliot, Gil. *Twentieth Century Book of the Dead.* London: Allen Lane, 1972. 242 pp.

Until recently this was the only work in English that tried to calculate totals for all deaths from war and democide in the twentieth century. In many of the statistics, the two are lumped together, and usually no sources are given for them. Moreover, the usefulness of many of the subclassifications are questionable, such as those killed by "small guns" versus "big guns." However, as a pioneering effort, it breaks new ground and provides a helpful context for understanding a major democide by trying to see it through the eyes of an average victim. It concludes that major twentieth-century violence has caused 110 million deaths (p. 215), which in the light of current research is much too low.

Foreign Affairs Research Institute. *The Current Death Toll of International Communism.* London: Arrow House, 1979. 12 pp.

Details, with citations, the democide in each communist state and concludes that the toll "could not be lower than 70 million and must number at some point up to twice that conservative minimum" (p. 11).

Harff, Barbara, and Ted Robert Gurr. "Toward Empirical Theory of Genocides and Politicides: Identification and Measurement of Cases Since 1945." *International Studies Quarterly* 32, no. 3 (1988): 359–71.

Pursuant to developing a typology of democide, the authors provide (without sources) what is meant to be a comprehensive listing of democides since World War II. The list is limited, however, as can be seen from their total of seven million to sixteen million killed (p. 370), the high being near half of the number probably killed by Communist China since 1949. Nonetheless, this work is pioneering, and their list and typology useful.

Rummel, R. J. *Statistics of Democide.* Münster, Germany: Lit Verlag; Piscataway, NJ: Transaction Publishers, 1997.

Rummel lists all the relevant estimates, sources, and calculations for each of the case studies in *Death by Government* (1994) and all additional cases of lesser democides. His statistics for all governments, 1900–1987, total a midestimate of

169,198,000, with a low estimate of 76,543,000, and a high of 359,348,000. Using these statistics, Rummel carries out a variety of systematic analyses of their causes and conditions. He concludes that these data show with high probability that the more democratic a government and the freer its people, the less likely it will commit democide. He concludes that it is empirically true that power kills and absolute power kills absolutely.

Stewart-Smith, D. G. *The Defeat of Communism.* London: Ludgate Press, 1964. 482 pp.

A book-length narrative chronology of communism. Provides relevant war and democide statistics for periods in his chronology. Concludes that the communists killed 83,500,000 people in war and democide, excluding World War II (p. 223).

SOVIET UNION

From 1917 to 1987, the Communist Party of the Soviet Union and its various leaders murdered in one way or another 28,326,000 to 126,891,000 citizens and foreigners; the most conservative estimate would be 61,911,000 (54,767,000 citizens). The following general works shed light on this horrible and incredible democide, and many contain overall figures of their own that tend to confirm this total.

General Works

Heller, Mikhail, and Aleksandr Nekrich. *Utopia in Power: The History of the Soviet Union from 1917 to the Present.* Translated by Phyllis B. Carlos. New York: Summit Books, 1986. 877 pp.

One of the best histories of the Soviet Union, it provides insight into motives and processes, while being sensitive to the how, when, and what of democide.

Kravchenko, Victor. *I Chose Freedom: The Personal and Political Life of a Soviet Official.* New York: Scribner's, 1946. 496 pp.

This is an important book. It is the firsthand account of much of the party's thinking, democide, and related events by one intimately involved as an official. So damaging was the publication of this book that the Soviets launched a very effective propaganda and disinformation campaign against it.

Calculations of Soviet Democide

Conquest, Robert. *The Human Cost of Soviet Communism.* Washington, DC: U.S. Government Printing Office, 1970. 25 pp.

A very useful overview of Soviet killing and one of the few attempts to calculate overall Soviet democide. Conquest concludes by quoting the minimum of twenty million dead calculated in his *Great Terror* (see below) and then adds that at least several million would have to be added to the figure for the Stalin-Yezhov period.

Dyadkin, Iosif G. *Unnatural Deaths in the USSR, 1928–1954.* Translated by Tania Deruguine. New Brunswick, NJ: Transaction Books, 1983. 80 pp.

Until recently, this was the only book in English wholly devoted to determining Soviet democide. A former professor of geophysics at the All-Union Geophysical Research Institute, Kalinin, USSR, Dyadkin wrote this former *samizdat* (underground literature) based on "census" returns. He calculated that for the years between 1926 and 1954, repression cost 26,000,000 to 35,450,000 lives, excluding war dead (pp. 41, 48, 55, 60). For the same period, he determined that the population deficit was 78,000,000, including unborn (p. 59). For this *samizdat* he was imprisoned in the gulag for three years.

Maximoff, G. P. *The Guillotine at Work: Twenty Years of Terror in Russia (Data and Documents)*. Chicago: Chicago Section of the Alexander Berkman Fund, 1940. 624 pp.

An important and statistics-filled attempt to document Lenin's democide in the years immediately following the Bolshevik coup in 1917. For example, Maximoff calculates a democide of at least seventy thousand in 1921, including a "most conservative" thirty thousand to forty thousand executed (p. 199). This is an eye-opener for those who insist that Lenin had little blood on his hands.

Rummel, R. J. *Lethal Politics: Soviet Genocide and Mass Murder Since 1917*. New Brunswick, NJ : Transaction Publishers, 1990. 268 pp.

A historical and statistical analysis of Soviet democide. Concludes that 61,911,000 people probably were killed, including 54,767,000 citizens.

Stalin and His Period

In the bloody history of the Soviet Union, Stalin's reign from 1928 to 1953 was the most ruthless. At an absolute minimum, he and his henchmen murdered at least 19,641,000 people through terror, deportations, gulag, the intentional Ukrainian famine, purges, and collectivization, and possibly as many as 91,685,000. A most reasonable figure is probably around 42,672,000. The following studies focus particularly on Stalin, but relevant figures also are given by most of the general or topical studies listed for the Soviet Union.

Antonov-Ovseenko, Anton. *The Time of Stalin: Portrait of a Tyranny*. Translated by George Saunders. New York: Harper & Row, 1981. 374 pp.

An in-depth treatment and analysis of this period, with helpful information on Stalin's various democides. Antonov-Ovseenko claims that Stalin killed thirty million to forty million people (p. 126).

Conquest, Robert. *The Great Terror: Stalin's Purge of the Thirties.* New York: Macmillan, 1968. 633 pp.

A thorough investigation into the background, reasons, and consequences of Stalin's great purge of the Communist Party from 1937 to 1938 in which perhaps one million people were executed (p. 532). Packed with details and useful information on the 1930s. Conquest presents an appendix in which he carefully considers diverse evidence on the human toll under Stalin and finds that for twenty-three years of his rule, "we get a figure of 20 million dead, which is almost certainly too low and might require an increase of 50 percent or so" (p. 533). This is perhaps the most widely quoted figure about Soviet democide in the literature.

Conquest, Robert. *The Great Terror: A Reassessment.* New York: Oxford University Press, 1990. 570 pp.

Based on the most recent information revealed as a result of greater freedom of access in the Soviet Union, Conquest reconsiders the above calculated democide under Stalin and, without explicitly altering his above estimate, concludes that "the sheer magnitudes of the Stalin holocaust are now beyond doubt" (p. 487).

Medvedev, Roy A. *On Stalin and Stalinism.* Translated by Ellen de Kadt. Oxford: Oxford University Press, 1979. 205 pp.

As a judicious and insightful analysis of Soviet communism and Stalin's period by a Marxist historian, this work is an important corrective to the work of many Western Sovietologists.

Medvedev cites demographer M. Maksudov's claim that from 1918 to 1953 there were twenty-two million to twenty-three million unnatural deaths (pp. 140–41).

Tolstoy, Nikolai. *Stalin's Secret War.* New York: Holt, Rinehart and Winston, 1981. 463 pp.

A fact-filled and democide-sensitive analysis of Stalin's period and a good source of different kinds of democide statistics.

Gulag

The concentration and forced-labor camps, the system of which is now known as the gulag, were the most lethal Soviet institutions. Their major product was death and only secondarily labor. Established by Lenin, the camps were vastly developed by Stalin such that in the post–World War II period, they contained perhaps 12,000,000 prisoners, even possibly 20,000,000. The overall toll in the gulag, including those dying in transit to or between camps, was probably from 15,919,000 to 82,281,000 prisoners, most likely 39,464,000. The following works help substantiate these figures while providing a feel for the slow and miserable deaths underlying these figures.

Applebaum, Anne, and Magdalena Chocano. *Gulag/Gulag: A History.* Barcelona: Debate Editorial, 2004.

In this impressive, first fully documented history of the gulag, the authors believe that over sixty years, nearly thirty million prisoners passed through the Soviet Gulag. They show through personal stories and archival material what a deadly and dehumanizing system the gulag was. And they especially document what in the West is little understood: the economic function this forced-labor system served. It was a communist state–run business in which people were of no consequence and were worked to death.

Conquest, Robert. *Kolyma: The Arctic Death Camps.* New York: Viking Press, 1978. 254 pp.

A must read. This is a chilling and detailed history of the forced-labor mining camps in Kolyma (northeastern Siberia). Life expectancy in some of these camps was measured in months; in some no one survived. The overall death rate was 25 percent per year (p. 220); Conquest calculates that from the 1930s to the 1950s, two million to five and a half million died in these camps alone (pp. 227–28).

Kosyk, Volodymyr. *Concentration Camps in the USSR.* London: Ukrainian Publishers, 1962.

This is a careful statistical analysis of the number of prisoners in the camps and the approximate number of deaths for each year from 1927 to 1958. Kosyk concludes that 32,600,000 died in the camps, but he also warns that this figure is probably too low (p. 79).

Panin, Dimitri. *The Notebooks of Sologdin.* Translated by John Moore. New York: Harcourt Brace Jovanovich, 1976. 320 pp.

Written by a mechanical engineer who spent more than a dozen years in the camps, this is an excellent analysis of Soviet democide and particularly of the gulag. Panin estimates that 2,000,000 to 3,000,000 people were murdered from 1922 to 1928 (p. 93n), a period that many Sovietologists claim was relatively free of terror and mass killing. Overall, from 1917 to 1953, Panin estimates the democide at 57,000,000 to 69,500,000 people (p. 93n).

Solzhenitsyn, Aleksandr I. *The Gulag Archipelago 1918–1956: An Experiment in Literary Investigation.* Vols. 1–2. Translated by Thomas P. Whitney. New York: Harper & Row, 1973. 660 pp.

This and the following two volumes not only have received international acclaim for their personal, historical, and analytical description of gulag, but they caused many Westerners to reconsider their pro-communism or sympathy for the Soviet Union. These must be read by anyone wishing to get a feel for the camps, their administration, the sheer misery, and the widespread deaths that occurred. Of particular note is that the camps are treated as part of a process, beginning with the very nature of communist rule, its terror, the arrest, torture and sentencing, prison, transit to the camps, life and death in the camps, administrative resentencing, and for survivors, conditional release.

Solzhenitsyn, Aleksandr I. *The Gulag Archipelago 1918–1956: An Experiment in Literary Investigation.* Vols. 3–4. Translated by Thomas P. Whitney. New York: Harper & Row, 1975. 712 pp.

Solzhenitsyn cites a professor of statistics who claims that "internal repression" cost 66,000,000 lives (p. 10).

Solzhenitsyn, Aleksandr I. *The Gulag Archipelago 1918–1956: An Experiment in Literary Investigation.* Vols. 5–7. Translated by Harry Willetts. New York: Harper & Row, 1978. 558 pp.

Zorin, Libushe. *Soviet Prisons and Concentration Camps: An Annotated Bibliography 1917–1980.* Newtonville, MA: Oriental Research Partners, 1980. 118 pp.

Ukraine Famine

From 1932 to 1933, Stalin purposely starved to death five million (maybe even ten million) Ukrainians, probably to

suppress Ukrainian nationalism and destroy peasant opposition to collectivism. Many works have recently been
published on this, and only the most noteworthy can be
listed here. Several excellent studies are also included in
the general works listed earlier at the beginning of this
bibliography.

Conquest, Robert. *The Harvest of Sorrow: Soviet Collectivization
and the Terror-Famine.* New York: Oxford University Press,
1986. 412 pp.

This is the best work on the famine. It gives details and evidence not widely available. Conquest carefully considers
whether the famine was in fact intentional, and after weighing
opposing arguments, he concludes that it had to be. He also
evaluates separate estimates of the toll and gives his reasoning
for selecting his estimate that five million died in the Ukraine
(p. 306).

Dalrymple, Dana G. *The Soviet Famine of 1932–1934.* Soviet Studies 15, no. 3 (1964): 250–84.

Perhaps the first scholarly study published on the famine that
views it as intentional. Dalrymple compares a variety of estimates of the toll and accepts a figure around five million for
the famine in and outside the Ukraine (p. 250).

Mace, James E. "Famine and Nationalism in Soviet Ukraine."
Problems of Communism (May-June 1984): 37–50.

An excellent presentation of the information on the famine
and its context. Mace argues that, according to accepted international definitions, this famine was genocide (p. 37). Using
demographic statistics, he calculates that seven and a half million Ukrainians died as a result (p. 39).

Serbyn, Roman, and Bohdan Krawchenko, eds. *Famine in Ukraine, 1932–1933*. Downsview, ON: University of Toronto Press, 1986.

A collection of factual and significant studies on the famine.

World War II Repatriation

Tolstoy, Nikolai. *Victims of Yalta*. Rev. ed. London: Corgi Books, 1979. 640 pp.

This is a detailed historical study of the forced repatriation of Soviet citizens *and others* into Soviet hands by the Allies as World War II came to an end and after. Some 5,500,000 people were repatriated, among whom (based on Tolstoy's statistics) perhaps 825,000 to 1,100,000 were killed (pp. 515–16), many within hours of being repatriated.

Treatment of Occupied or Absorbed Nations

Conquest, Robert. *The Nation Killers: The Soviet Deportation of Nationalities*. London: Macmillan, 1970. 222 pp.

A revision of an earlier work (*The Soviet Deportation of Nationalities* [1960]), Conquest offers a balanced description of the deportation of Soviet national and ethnic groups during World War II, including a conservative analysis of the numbers deported and their deaths. In total, 1,850,000 people from eight national and ethnic groups were deported (pp. 65–66), with a likely 530,000 dying as a result (p. 162).

Gross, Jan T. *Revolution from Abroad: The Soviet Conquest of Poland's Western Ukraine and Western Belorussia*. Princeton, NJ: Princeton University Press, 1988. 334 pp.

A description of the Soviet rape of Poland from 1939 to 1940, mass murder of Poles, and the deportation of 1,250,000 others (p. 146) to inhospitable parts of the Soviet Union; through September 1941, 300,000 Poles died from deportation and in concentration camps (p. 229).

Misiunas, Romuald J., and Rein Taagepera. *The Baltic States: Years of Dependence 1940–1980*. Berkeley and Los Angeles: University of California Press, 1983. 333 pp.

An excellent history of the Soviet occupation of the Baltic States. Gives a statistical appendix, which includes figures on war and occupation deaths from 1940 to 1945 (with a "very approximate 'questimate'" of 550,000 dead). Also presents information on the deportation of Balts in which many died, perhaps more than 100,000 in 1949 and after (p. 100).

COMMUNIST CHINA

General

In the magnitude of its killing, Communist China surpasses the Soviet Union. Since they formerly seized power in 1949 and up to 1987, the Chinese communists killed 43,999,000 to 140,671,000 people (most likely 73,236,000), counting the toll of the great famine of 1959/60, which killed perhaps 38,000,000, but not counting the 3,466,000 killed by the communists before they assumed total control. The following works particularly help understand this democide and provide supporting statistics.

Chang, Jung. *Wild Swans: Three Daughters of China*. New York: Touchstone, 2003.

Chang recounts the stories of three generations of her family in China and how they fared under communism, rose to power in the Communist Party, and were destroyed in its Cultural Revolution. The book well communicates the emotions and horrors her family went through, and its heartbreak. A must read to understand China in the twentieth century.

Chou, Ching-wen. *Ten Years of Storm: The True Story of the Communist Regime in China.* Translated and edited by Lai Ming. New York: Holt, Rinehart and Winston, 1960. 323 pp.

Chu, Valentin. *Ta Ta, Tan Tan: The Inside Story of Communist China.* New York: Norton, 1963. 320 pp. [*Ta ta, tan tan* means "fight fight, talk talk."]

Garside, Roger. *Coming Alive: China After Mao.* New York: McGraw-Hill, 1981. 458 pp.

Guillermaz, Jacques. *The Chinese Communist Party in Power, 1949–1976.* Translated by Anne Destenay. Boulder, CO: Westview Press, 1976. 614 pp.

Hunter, Edward. *The Black Book on China: The Continuing Revolt.* New York: Bookmailer, 1958. 136 pp.

Hunter believes the communist democide to be closer to fifty million than to thirty million (p. 137).

Labin, Suzanne. *The Anthill: The Human Condition in Communist China.* Translated by Edward Fitzgerald. New York: Praeger, 1960. 442 pp.

Tang, Peter S. H., and Joan M. Maloney. *Communist China: The Domestic Scene, 1949–1967.* South Orange, NJ: Seton Hall University Press, 1967. 606 pp.

Calculations of Overall Democide

Li, Cheng-Chung. *The Question of Human Rights on China Main-land.* Republic of China: World Anti-Communist League, China Chapter, 1979. 180 pp.

A description of the various ways in which communists have violated human rights. Based on statistics from the Republic of China, the author calculates the democide as 78,860,000 peo-ple for 1949 to 1968, not counting the Korean War and guer-rilla dead (p. 153).

Rummel, R. J. *China's Bloody Century: Genocide and Mass Murder Since 1900.* New Brunswick, NJ: Transaction Publishers, 1991. 333 pp.

Presents an historical and statistical analysis of communist de-mocide from 1928 to 1987. Finds that the democide by the People's Republic of China probably amounted to 35,236,000 killed (excluding the 38,000,000 dead in Mao's Great Famine, which Rummel subsequently concluded was democide and added to the total).

Shalom, Stephen Rosskamm. *Deaths in China Due to Communism: Propaganda Versus Reality.* Occasional Paper, no. 15. Tempe: Arizona State University, 1984. 234 pp.

A must study for anyone interested in China's overall demo-cide. This is a careful and detailed line-by-line critique of Walker's democide statistics (see below), which Shalom con-cludes are far too high. Rather, he calculates that three million to four million were killed from 1949 to 1970 (p. 111).

Walker, Richard L. *The Human Cost of Communism in China.* Wash-ington, DC: U.S. Government Printing Office, 1971. 28 pp.

Walker outlines the nature of Communist Chinese democide and also gives a widely quoted table of democide organized by type, which adds up to a total (ignoring Korean War dead) of 31,750,000 to 58,500,000 killed between 1949 to 1970 (p. 16).

Mao Tse-tung

Chang, Jung, and Jon Halliday. *Mao: The Unknown Story.* New York: Anchor, 2006.

Chang grew up in China during the Cultural Revolution, and her family was highly placed in the Communist Party. This eye-opening biography of Mao is based on Chang and Halliday's extensive archival research in China and Russia, Chang's interviews with former high officials, and her own experience and that of her family. They conclude that Mao was responsible for the Korean War, maneuvered to dominate the global communist movement and ultimately the world. They say that the human toll under Mao's tyrannical rule was well over seventy million.

Mao Tse-tung. *Selected Works of Mao Tse-tung.* 4 vols. Peking, China: Foreign Languages Press, 1967.

This collection contains many selections that are essential reading for understanding the background of Mao's later policies and the underlying rationale for the associated democide.

Paloczi-Horvath, George. *Mao Tse-Tung: Emperor of the Blue Ants.* New York: Doubleday, 1963. 393 pp.

Gulag

From 1949 to 1987, possibly as many as 15,720,000 Chinese died in forced-labor camps. Unlike the Soviet gulag, there are few works on the Chinese camps system. Following are some of the most relevant.

Bao Ruo-Wang (Jean Pasqualini), and Rudolph Chelminski. *Prisoner of Mao.* New York: Coward, McCann and Geoghegan, 1973.

International Commission Against Concentration Camp Practices. *White Book on Forced Labour and Concentration Camps in the People's Republic of China.* 2 vols. Paris: Commission Internationale Contre Le Regime Concentrationnaire, 1957–58.

Whyte, Martin King. "Corrective Labor Camps in China." *Asian Survey* 13, no. 3 (March 1973): 253–69.

Cultural Revolution

From 1964 to 1968, during the height of the killing associated with the violent cultural revolution, some one million Chinese were murdered or otherwise killed. Few social revolutions have been as violent. The following works provide analysis and background for appreciating this democide and associated events.

Domes, Jurgen. *The Internal Politics of China, 1949–1972.* Translated by Rudiger Machetzki. New York: Praeger, 1973. 258 pp.

An informative analysis of the events and debate among the top leaders that led to and comprised the Cultural Revolution.

Liu, Guokai. *A Brief Analysis of the Cultural Revolution.* Armonk, NY: M. E. Sharpe, 1987. 151 pp.

An abridged translated version of the author's essay published in China, this is a first-rate analysis of the revolution by a participant.

Thurston, Anne F. *Enemies of the People.* New York: Knopf, 1987.

NAZI GERMANY

Stacks of volumes on Nazi Germany are available, many of them concerned with its history, diplomacy, politics, aggression, repression, and the Holocaust. Very few of them, however, consider the democide against non-Jews. Yet from 1933 to 1945 the Nazis probably murdered some 15,003,000 to 31,595,000 people (probably 20,946,000 overall), including 5,291,000 Jews. Only those works providing the most relevant statistics are noted below.

General

Berenbaum, Michael, ed. *Mosaic of Victims: Non-Jews Persecuted and Murdered by the Nazis.* New York: New York University Press, 1990. 244 pp.

This is an especially important collection of articles that covers topics and provides information not easily available in other works. For example, there are chapters on Nazi policies in Ukraine, the USSR proper, Poland, Belgium and France, as well as the Slavs, the Nazi euthanasia program, forced labor, pacifists, and Croatia.

Hirschfeld, Gerhard, ed. *The Policies of Genocide: Jews and Soviet Prisoners of War in Nazi Germany.* London: Allen & Unwin, 1986. 172 pp.

Kogon, Eugen. *The Theory and Practice of Hell: The German Concentration Camps and the System Behind Them.* Translated by Heinz Norden. New York: Farrar, Straus and Giroux, 2006. 343 pp.

Although relatively short in treatment, this gives a useful history and accounting of the Nazi concentration–death camp system. The chapter on the "statistics of mortality" gives a yearly breakdown of the concentration camp population and calculates the overall concentration–death camp death toll as 7,125,000 people.

Calculations of Democide

Rummel, R. J. *Democide: Nazi Genocides and Mass Murder.* New Brunswick, NJ: Transaction Publishers, 1993. 150 pp.

An attempt to outline and explain Nazi democide and collect available statistics to calculate the overall toll, including that in occupied countries. Rummel finds that 20,946,000 people probably were murdered by the Nazis; this figure includes Jews, Gypsies, Poles, Russians, Yugoslavs, Frenchmen, and many others.

Wytwycky, Bohdan. *The Other Holocaust: Many Circles of Hell.* Washington, DC: Novak Report on the New Ethnicity, 1980. 93 pp.

Wytwycky tries to explain and calculate the overall Nazi democide, especially on the Slavs. He concludes that 15,450,000 to 16,300,000 Jews, Gypsies, Soviet POWs, Ukrainians, Poles, and Byelorrussians were murdered (pp. 91–92).

Holocaust: Genocide of the Jews

Among the many works on the Holocaust, the following have been selected for the detail and excellence of their treatment, the understanding they provide to a non-Holocaust scholar, and the usefulness of their calculations of the total genocide.

Bauer, Yehuda. *A History of the Holocaust.* New York: Franklin Watts, 1982. 398 pp.

Presents a thorough history of the Holocaust and related events, with pertinent statistical tables; touches also on other genocides. Gives a country-by-country breakdown of the Holocaust, which Bauer estimates totals 5,820,960 Jews murdered (p. 335).

Dawidowicz, Lucy S. *The War Against the Jews, 1933–1945.* New York: Holt, Rinehart and Winston, 1975. 460 pp.

In addition to a general analysis and history of the genocide, Dawidowicz also gives an appendix providing a brief account for each country of what happened to the Jews and the death toll, which overall equals 5,933,900 murdered (p. 403).

Fein, Helen. *Accounting for Genocide: National Responses and Jewish Victimization During the Holocaust.* New York: Free Press, 1979. 468 pp.

A unique and careful social science and statistical attempt (including the use of multiple regression) to explain the Holocaust. There is much important information of value given in its various tables, themselves well worth separate study. Fein calculates that 4,610,000 Jews were lost (p. 21), not counting the USSR (p. 21).

Fein, Helen. "Reviewing the Toll: Jewish Dead, Losses and Victims of the Holocaust." *Shoah* 2, no. 2 (1981): 20–26.

Fein compares a variety of estimates of the Holocaust's toll and tries to account for their differences. Concludes, "All sources suggest the likelihood that competent estimates will fall . . . between five and six million" (p. 23).

Fleming, Gerald. *Hitler and the Final Solution.* Berkeley and Los Angeles: University of California Press, 1984. 219 pp.

Gives a country-by-country breakdown of the genocide toll, which he estimates to be 4,975,477 murdered (p. 193).

Gilbert, Martin. *The Macmillan Atlas of the Holocaust.* New York: Macmillan, 1982. 256 pp.

An excellent collection of maps on a variety of aspects of the genocide, including where anti-Jewish pogroms and persecutions have occurred, Poland's major Jewish communities, the destruction of Croatian Jews, deportations and revolt, death camps, and the Jews of Bessarabia. Many of the maps also give statistics, and one in particular maps the toll by each country that equals slightly more than 5,750,000 (pp. 244–45).

Gutman, Israel, and Robert Rozett. "Estimated Jewish Losses in the Holocaust." In *Encyclopedia of the Holocaust,* edited by Israel Gutman. 4 vols. New York: Macmillan, 1990. 4:1797–1802.

Gutman analyzes the Jewish losses by country and totals them as 5,596,029 to 5,860,129 (p. 1799).

Hilberg, Raul. *The Destruction of the European Jews.* Rev. ed. New York: Holmes & Meier, 1985. 1273 pp.

Deservedly, this is perhaps the most quoted work on the genocide. Historically and statistically thorough. In appendix 3, Hilberg tabulates a statistical recapitulation by killing operation and country, totaling 5,100,000 Jews murdered.

Reitlinger, Gerald. *The Final Solution: The Attempt to Exterminate the Jews of Europe, 1939–1945.* 2nd rev. ed. London: Vallentine, Mitchell, and Co., 1968. 668 pp.

Appendix 1 provides a country-by-country statistical summary and analysis of the genocide. Reitlinger "conjectures" that 4,204,400 to 4,575,400 Jews were thus murdered (p. 546), the lowest count by any reputable study.

Slavs

Dallin, Alexander. *German Rule in Russia, 1941–1945: A Study of Occupation Policies.* 2nd rev. ed. New York: Macmillan, 1981. 707 pp.

Must reading for an understanding of Nazi democide in the Soviet Union. The book is historically and analytically thorough.

Gross, Jan Tomasz. *Polish Society Under German Occupation: The Generalgouvernement, 1939–1944*. Princeton, NJ: Princeton University Press, 1979. 343 pp.

Kamenetsky, Ihor. *Secret Nazi Plans for Eastern Europe: A Study of Lebensraum Policies*. New York: Bookman, 1961. 263 pp.

Gypsies

Kenrick, Donald, and Grattan Puxon. *The Destiny of Europe's Gypsies*. New York: Basic Books, 1972. 256 pp.

This is a major and rare work on the Nazi genocide of the Gypsies. The authors give the overall toll as 219,700 Gypsies murdered (p. 184).

Trynauer, Gabrielle. *Gypsies and the Holocaust: A Bibliography and Introductory Essay*. Montreal: Interuniversity Center for European Studies and the Montreal Institute for Genocide Studies, 1989. 51 pp.

Homosexuals

Porter, Jack Nusan. *Sexual Politics in the Third Reich: The Persecution of the Homosexuals During the Holocaust: A Bibliography and Introductory Essay*. Newton, MA: Spencer Press, 1991.

An annotated bibliography of German- and English-language materials on sex, homosexuality, and the Nazis.

Rector, Frank. *The Nazi Extermination of Homosexuals*. New York: Stein and Day, 1981. 189 pp.

One of the few major works in English on the Nazi treatment of homosexuals, which amounted to genocide. He concludes that at least five hundred thousand homosexuals were murdered (p. 116).

MILITARIST JAPAN

No major general works on genocide and mass murder discuss the massacres and atrocities of militarized and totalitarian Japan. Yet just considering World War II and the Sino-Japanese War (1937–45), the Japanese democide probably amounted to 3,017,000 to 9,488,000 people (most likely 5,890,000). This is surely the forgotten democide.

General

Dower, John W. *War Without Mercy: Race and Power in the Pacific War.* New York: Pantheon Books, 1986. 398 pp.

This is an excellent and comprehensive nonmilitary work on the Pacific War. It not only includes much material relevant to various Japanese democides, as in China and Indonesia, but also includes an extensive discussion of the American side of the war and U.S. atrocities. Dower argues that this was a racial war for Americans.

James, David H. *The Rise and Fall of the Japanese Empire.* London: George Allen & Unwin, 1951. 409 pp.

A most helpful analytical description and analysis of the Japanese Empire and particularly of the Japanese treatment of Western POWs by a scholar who was a prisoner of the Japanese himself.

Kerr, E. Bartlett. *Surrender and Survival: The Experience of American POWs in the Pacific, 1941–1945.* New York: Morrow, 1985. 356 pp.

Pritchard, R. John, and Sonia Magbanua Zaide, eds. *The Tokyo War Crimes Trial.* 22 vols. New York: Garland Publishing, 1981.

The complete transcripts of the proceedings of the International Military Tribunal for the Far East. This is a first source for serious study of Japanese democide, and it is an excellent collection of testimony and facts. Included is an excellent index, which contains items on massacres and atrocities.

Williams, Peter, and David Wallace. *Unit 731: The Japanese Army's Secret of Secrets*. London: Hodder & Stoughton, 1989. 366 pp.

An account of the Japanese development of bacteriological weapons, from their testing stage to actual field-testing in China. Gives limited information on numbers killed, but includes essential information on the how and why.

Sino-Japanese War

Most of Japan's democide was against the Chinese during the 1937–45 Sino-Japanese War. The Japanese murdered 3,949,000 Chinese (a conservative estimate). There are no works on this democide per se, although the following and the above volumes provide some understanding.

Dorn, Frank. *The Sino-Japanese War, 1937–41: From Marco Polo Bridge to Pearl Harbor*. New York: Macmillan, 1974. 477 pp.

Timperley, H. J. *Japanese Terror in China*. New York: Modern Age Books, 1938. 220 pp.

KHMER ROUGE CAMBODIA

It is now well known that the communist Khmer Rouge committed an incredible democide in Cambodia once they grabbed power in 1975. Most published collections on genocide now include a chapter on Cambodia. Considering the various estimates of the toll, from six hundred thousand to three million were murdered during their reign (probably two million Cambodians overall, close to a third of the population). The following are the best studies giving a foundation for understanding this incredible figure.

Barron, John, and Anthony Paul. *Peace with Horror: The Untold Story of Communist Genocide in Cambodia.* London: Hodder and Stoughton, 1977. 234 pp. [American edition: *Murder of a Gentle Land.* New York: Reader's Digest Press; Thomas Y. Crowell]

Based on refugee reports, this was among the first and most influential reports of the horror and mass killing under the Khmer Rouge in its first eighteen months. It is detailed and close to the experience of the average Cambodian. Barron and Paul estimate the democide toll as 1,200,000 in the first twenty-one months (p. 206), which they subsequently believed much too low.

Becker, Elizabeth. *When the War Was Over: Cambodia's Revolution and the Voices of Its People.* New York: Simon & Shuster, 1986. 501 pp.

This is an excellent starting point on the Khmer Rouge period by a reporter who covered the war in Cambodia for the *Washington Post.* Becker claims that two million died at the hands of the Khmer Rouge (pp. 19–20).

Jackson, Karl D., ed. *Cambodia, 1975–1978: Rendezvous with Death.* Princeton, NJ: Princeton University Press, 1989, 334 pp.

A collection of first-rate articles by experts on the Khmer Rouge period, particularly focusing on the context for understanding the Khmer Rouge, the dynamics of power among them, and the nature and consequences of their economic politics. Contains translations of important Khmer Rouge documents.

Kampuchean Inquiry Commission. *Kampuchea in the Seventies: Report of a Finnish Inquiry Commission.* Helsinki, Finland: Kampuchean Inquiry Commission, 1982. 114 pp.

A detailed investigation into conditions under the Khmer Rouge. Gives the toll as nearly one million people (p. 35).

Kiernan, Ben, and Chanthou Boua. *Peasants and Politics in Kampuchea, 1942–1981.* London: Zed Press, 1982. 401 pp.

This has become a classic collection of relevant, in-depth scholarly studies that provide a helpful background for understanding the Khmer Rouge and their rule. It is particularly helpful in understanding the material and social conditions of the peasantry, the communist movement, and Pol Pot's role. Also useful for perspective and context are the large number of testimonies from Cambodians who lived under the Khmer Rouge.

Ponchaud, François. *Cambodia Year Zero.* Translated by Nancy Amphoux. New York: Holt, Rinehart and Winston, 1977. 212 pp.

A report on what happened under the Khmer Rouge in its first year or so by a Frenchman who lived among Cambodian peasants and is fluent in the language. This independently complements the above work by Barron and Paul. Ponchaud estimates the early democide toll as "certainly" more than 1,000,000 (p. 71).

Democide

Kiernan, Ben. "The Genocide in Cambodia, 1975–79." *Bulletin of Concerned Asian Scholars* 22, no. 2 (1990): 35–40.

Responding to Michael Vickery's critique ("Democratic Kampuchea—CIA to the Rescue," below) of the CIA article (*Kampuchea: A Demographic Catastrophe,* below), Kiernan provides more calculations on the Cham genocide and then outlines the genocide against other groups in Cambodia and presents statistics on the overall democide. He estimates this as 1,500,000 (p. 38).

Kiernan, Ben. "Orphans of Genocide: The Cham Muslims of Kampuchea Under Pol Pot." *Bulletin of Concerned Asian Scholars* 20, no. 4 (1988): 2–33.

This is a scholarly and detailed account of the Khmer Rouge genocide against the Chams by a first-rate scholar on Cambodia. Out of some 250,000 Chams in 1975 (p. 6), Kiernan estimates that 90,000 were killed (p. 30).

U.S. Central Intelligence Agency. *Kampuchea: A Demographic Catastrophe.* Washington, DC: U.S. Central Intelligence Agency, 1980. 14 pp.

This is a widely quoted attempt by the CIA to determine from demographic statistics the extent of the death toll under the Khmer Rouge. They calculate the absolute population decline under the Khmer Rouge as 1,200,000 to 1,800,000 (p. 5).

Vickery, Michael. "Democratic Kampuchea—CIA to the Rescue." *Bulletin of Concerned Asian Scholars* 14 (October–December 1982): 45–54.

This is a hostile but important critique of the above CIA report. Vickery calculates that the CIA estimate of 1,300,000 dead should be reduced to about 290,000 to 425,000 (p. 54), figures he subsequently admits are much too low.

COMMUNIST VIETNAM

The mass murder and country-wide killing by the Vietnamese communists from 1945 through the 1980s has been totally ignored among students of genocide, doubtless in part because of the confusion of much of this killing with the casualties of the Vietnam War, not to mention the controversies engendered by that war. However, the major part of this democide occurred before and after the war. In any case, from 1945 to 1987 the North Vietnamese (which controlled all Vietnam after April 1975) murdered from 715,000 to 3,657,000 (probably 1,659,000 people, 944,000 of them Vietnamese).

General

Canh, Nguyen Van. *Vietnam Under Communism, 1975–1982.* Stanford, CA: Hoover Institution Press, 1983. 312 pp.

Canh, a Vietnamese and former law professor, presents an important description and analysis of life in Vietnam after the North Vietnamese takeover of the South. Must reading for an assessment of this period and its democide.

Chi, Hoang Van. *From Colonialism to Communism: A Case History of North Vietnam.* New York: Praeger, 1964. 252 pp.

Based on personal experience and extensive research, the work by a Vietnamese nationalist gives a detailed account of the communist suppression of the nationalist movement and consolidation of power in the North after 1945 and the subsequent land reform and party purges. This is essential reading for understanding the associated democide. Chi believes that 500,000 Vietnamese were "sacrificed" in the land reform campaign of 1953 to 1956 (pp. 72, 205).

Lewy, Guenter. *America in Vietnam.* New York: Oxford University Press, 1978. 540 pp.

Among the best and most balanced works on the Vietnam War, Lewy also provides information on communist democide in the South during the war and judiciously weighs allegations of extensive American massacres and atrocities.

Democide

Desbarats, Jacqueline. "Repression in the Socialist Republic of Vietnam: Executions and Population Relocation." In *The Vietnam Debate: A Fresh Look at the Arguments,* edited by John Norton Moore, 193–201. New York: University Press of America, 1990.

Based on extensive interviews of Vietnamese refugees, Desbarats reports her discovery and surprise at the extent of executions in Vietnam after the war. She concludes that more than one hundred thousand people must have been executed (p. 197).

Hosmer, Stephen. *Viet Cong Repression and Its Implications for the Future.* Lexington, MA: Heath, 1970. 176 pp.

This is a study of the communist use of terror and repression as a method of revolutionary warfare. It helps to understand why democide was seen as a legitimate tool and the extent and variety of its uses during the Vietnam War.

U.S. Senate, 92nd Congress, 2nd Session, Committee on the Judiciary. *The Human Cost of Communism in Vietnam.* Washington, DC: U.S. Government Printing Office, 1972. 119 pp.

This compiles excerpts of publications that describe North Vietnamese democide and presents relevant analyses. The aim is to predict the bloodbath that would occur in case of the North's victory in the Vietnam War.

Wiesner, Louis. Victims and Survivors: *Displaced Persons and Other War Victims in Viet-Nam, 1954–1975.* Westport, CT: Greenwood Press, 1988. 448 pp.

This work by an internationally recognized expert on refugees gives the best overall view of the refugee problem during the

Vietnam War. It is full of statistics and facts and contains diverse information on the democide in the South by the North Vietnamese, such as attacks on refugee movements or camps.

Boat People

Since 1975, perhaps as many as one and a half million Vietnamese have fled Vietnam, many in rickety boats, risking storms and pirates in order to reach an uncertain haven. Many thus died at sea, perhaps five hundred thousand of them. This constitutes democide by Vietnam because those who died did so while fleeing for their lives. Virtually all that has been written on the so-called boat people is in newspapers or popular magazines. The following are among the few serious discussions of their flight and plight.

Cerquone, Joseph. "Uncertain Harbors: The Plight of Vietnamese Boat People." In *Issue Paper of the U.S. Committee for Refugees.* Washington, DC: American Council for Nationalities Service, 1987. 39 pp.

Hugo, Graeme. "Postwar Refugee Migration in Southeast Asia: Patterns, Problems, and Policies." In *Refugees: A Third World Dilemma,* edited by John R. Rigge, 237–52. Totowa, NJ: Rowman & Littlefield, 1987.

OTHER DEMOCIDE

Little has been written in English on the megamurders by other regimes. Attempts to determine the how, when, and why of democide in Communist North Korea, Afghanistan, Cuba, Ethiopia, Laos, Eastern Europe, Fascist Italy, fundamentalist Moslem Iran, and elsewhere is a matter of digging in the conventional histories and political studies or relevant newspaper and news magazine articles and specialized pieces. In North Korea, for example, possibly three million Koreans have been murdered since 1948, but even partially related studies of this in English are generally unavailable. Following are a few publications that focus on democide on World War II Yugoslavia.

Paris, Edmond. *Genocide in Satellite Croatia, 1941–1945: A Record of Racial and Religious Persecutions and Massacres.* Translated by Lois Perkins. Chicago: American Institute for Balkan Affairs, 1961. 322 pp.

Paris offers analysis, facts, and personal testimonials on the genocide of Serbians by Croatia under totalitarian Ustashi rule during the Second World War. While the book ignores the counterpart genocide of the Croatians carried out by the Serbs when the war was ending and afterward (see Prcela and Guldescu below), Paris establishes in horrible detail the extent of this mass murder. He claims that 750,000 were killed, almost all Serbs (pp. 4, 9, 211).

Prcela, John, and Stanko Guldescu, eds. *Operation Slaughterhouse: Eyewitness Accounts of Postwar Massacres in Yugoslavia.* Philadelphia: Dorrance, 1970. 557 pp.

This describes much of the democide of Croatians and others by Tito's communist (partisan) forces as World War II ended and gives eyewitness testimonials, often by survivors of particular massacres. Prcela and Guldescu ignore the genocide of the Serbs by the Croatians described in the above work. Prcela and a colleague calculated that six hundred thousand Croats were murdered by the Tito regime (p. 121).

DEMOCRATIC PEACE BIBLIOGRAPHY

ARTICLES AND CHAPTERS

Archibugi, Daniele. "Immanuel Kant, Cosmopolitan Law, and Peace." *European Journal of International Relations* 1, no. 4 (December 1995): 429–56.

Babst, Dean V. "Elective Governments: A Force for Peace." *Wisconsin Sociologist* 3, no. 1 (1964): 9–14.

———. "A Force for Peace." *Industrial Research* (April 1972): 55–58.

———, and William Eckhardt. "How Peaceful Are Democracies Compared to Other Countries?" *Peace Research* 24, no. 2 (August 1992): 51–56.

Bachteler, Tobias. "Explaining the Democratic Peace: The Evidence from Ancient Greece Reviewed." *Journal of Peace Research* 34, no. 3 (August 1997): 315–23. See rejoinder by Bruce Russett, ibid., 323–24.

Benoit, Kenneth. "Democracies Really Are More Pacific (In General): Reexamining Regime Type and War Involvement." *Journal of Conflict Resolution* 40, no. 5 (December 1996): 636–58.

Bliss, Harry, and Bruce Russett. "Democratic Trading Partners: The Liberal Connection, 1962–1989." *Journal of Politics* 60, no. 4 (1998): 1126–47.

Braumoeller, Bear F. "Deadly Doves: Liberal Nationalism and the Democratic Peace in the Soviet Successor States." *International Studies Quarterly* 41, no. 3 (September 1997): 375–402.

Bremer, Stuart A. "Advancing the Scientific Study of War." *International Interactions* 19, nos. 1–2 (1993): 1–26.

―――. "Dangerous Dyads: Conditions Affecting the Likelihood of Interstate War, 1816–1965." *Journal of Conflict Resolution* 36, no. 2 (June 1992): 309–41.

―――. "Democracy and Militarized Interstate Conflict, 1816–1965." *International Interactions* 18, no. 3 (1993): 231–49.

Brinkley, Douglas. "Democratic Enlargement: The Clinton Doctrine." *Foreign Policy* 106 (Spring 1997): 111–27.

Carothers, Thomas. "Democracy Promotion Under Clinton." *Washington Quarterly* 18, no. 4 (Autumn 1995): 13–28.

Chan, Steve. "Democracy and War: Some Thoughts on Future Research Agenda." *International Interactions* 18 no. 3 (1993): 205–13.

―――. "In Search of Democratic Peace: Problems and Promise." *Mershon International Studies Review* 41, no. 1 (May 1997): 59–91.

―――. "Mirror, Mirror on the War . . . Are Democratic States More Pacific?" *Journal of Conflict Resolution* 28 (1984): 617–48.

Chapman, Stephen. "Will a Democratic World Really Be More Peaceful?" *Creators Syndicate,* January 8, 1995.

Clinton, Bill. "American Foreign Policy and the Democratic Ideal." *Orbis* 37, no. 4 (Fall 1993): 651–60.

Codevilla, Angelo. "Birds of a Feather." *National Interest* 35 (Spring 1994): 58–64.

Cohen, Raymond. "Needed: A Disaggregate Approach to the Democratic-Peace Theory" (Reply to Russett and Ray response to Cohen, 1994). *Review of International Studies* 21, no. 3 (1995): 323–25.

————. "Pacific Unions: A Reappraisal of the Theory That 'Democracies Do Not Go to War with Each Other." *Review of International Studies* 20 (1994): 207–23.

Czempiel, Ernst-Otto. "Governance and Democratization." In *Governance Without Government: Order and Change in World Politics,* edited by James N. Rosenau and Ernst-Otto Czempiel. Cambridge Studies in International Relations, no. 20. Cambridge, UK: Cambridge University Press, 1992.

Dixon, William J. "Democracy and the Management of International Conflict." *Journal of Conflict Resolution* 37, no. 1 (March 1993): 42–68.

————. "Democracy and the Peaceful Settlement of International Conflict." *American Political Science Review* 88, no. 1 (March 1994): 1–17.

Dizerega, Gus. "Democracies and Peace: The Self-Organizing Foundation for the Democratic Peace." *Review of Politics* 57, no. 2 (Spring 1995): 279–308.

Doyle, Michael W. "Kant, Liberal Legacies, and Foreign Affairs, Part I." *Philosophy and Public Affairs* 12 (Summer 1983): 205–235. Part 2, Ibid., 323–53.

————. "Liberalism and the End of the Cold War." In *International Relations Theory and the End of the Cold War,* edited by Richard Ned Lebow and Thomas Risse-Kappen. New York: Columbia University Press, 1995.

————. "Liberalism and World Politics." *American Political Science Review* 80, no. 4 (December 1986): 1151–69.

————. "Michael Doyle on the Democratic Peace." *International Security* 19, no. 4 (Spring 1995): 180–84.

————. "To the Editors" (Correspondence on the Democratic Peace). *International Security* 19, no. 4 (Spring 1995): 180–84.

———. "The Voice of the People: Political Theorists on the International Implications of Democracy." In *The Fall of Great Powers: Peace, Stability, and Legitimacy,* edited by Geir Lundestad. Oslo, Norway: Scandinavian University Press, 1994.

Ember, Carol, Melvin Ember, and Bruce Russett. "Peace Between Participatory Polities: A Cross-Cultural Test of the 'Democracies Rarely Fight Each Other' Hypothesis." *World Politics* 44, no. 4 (1992): 573–99.

Engelhardt, Michael. "Democracies, Dictatorships and Counterinsurgency: Regime Type Really Matter?" *Conflict Quarterly* 12, no. 3 (1992): 52–63.

Enterline, Andrew J. "Driving While Democratizing (DWD)." *International Security* 41, no. 3 (Spring 1996): 183–96. Response to Mansfield and Snyder (1995).

———." Regime Changes, Neighborhoods, and Interstate Conflict, 1816–1992." *Journal of Conflict Resolution* 42, no. 6 (December 1998): 804–29.

Farber, Henry S., and Joanne Gowa. "Polities and Peace." *International Security* 20, no. 2 (Fall 1995): 123–46.

Forsythe, David P. "Democracy, War, and Covert Action." *Journal of Peace Research* 29, no. 4 (November 1992): 385–95.

Garnham, David. "War-Proneness, War-Weariness, and Regime Type: 1816–1980." *Journal of Peace Research* 23 (1986): 279–89.

Gartzke, Erik. "Kant We All Just Get Along? Opportunity, Willingness, and the Origins of the Democratic Peace." *American Journal of Political Science* 42, no. 1 (1998): 1–27.

———. "Preferences and the Democratic Peace." *International Studies Quarterly* 44, no. 2 (2000): 191–212.

Gates, Scott, Torbjørn L. Knutsen, and Jonathon W. Moses. "Democracy and Peace: A More Skeptical View." *Journal of Peace Research* 33, no. 1 (1996): 1–10.

Gaubatz, Kurt. "Democratic States and Commitment in International Relations." *International Organization* 50, no. 1 (Winter 1996): 109–39.

———. "Election Cycles and War." *Journal of Conflict Resolution* 35, no. 2 (June 1991): 214–44.

———. "Kant, Democracy, and History." *Journal of Democracy* 7, no. 4 (October 1996): 136–50.

Geva, Nehemia, Karl Derouen, and Alex Mintz. "The Political Incentive Explanation of the 'Democratic Peace': Evidence from Experimental Research." *International Interactions* 18, no. 3 (1993): 215–29.

Gleditsch, Kristian S., and Michael D. Ward. "War and Peace in Space and Time: The Role of Democratization." *International Studies Quarterly* 44, no. 1 (March 2000): 1–29.

Gleditsch, Nils-Petter. "Democracy and Peace." *Journal of Peace Research* 29, no. 4 (1992): 369–76.

———. "Democracy and Peace: Good News for Human Rights Advocates." In *Broadening the Frontiers of Human Rights: Essays in Honor of Abjørn Eide,* edited by Donna Gomien, 287–307. Oslo: Scandinavian University Press, 1993.

———. "Democracy and the Future of European Peace." *European Journal of International Relations* 1, no. 4 (December 1995): 539–71.

———. "Focus On: Democracy and Peace." *Journal of Peace Research* 29, no. 4 (1992): 369–76.

———, and Håvard Hegre. "Peace and Democracy: Three Levels of Analysis." *Journal of Conflict Resolution* 41, no. 2 (1997): 283–310.

Gochman, Charles. Correspondence to the Editors on Democracy and Peace. *International Security* 21, no. 3 (Winter 1996): 177–87. Reply to Farber and Gowa, 1995.

———. "The Evolution of Disputes." *International Interactions* 19, nos. 1–2 (1993): 49–76.

————, and Zeev Maoz. "Militarized Interstate Disputes, 1816–1975: Procedures, Patterns, Insights." *Journal of Conflict Resolution* 28, no. 4 (December 1984): 585–615.

Gowa, Joanne. "Democratic States and International Disputes." *International Organization* 49, no. 3 (1995): 511–22.

Hagan, Joe D. "Domestic Political Systems and War Proneness." *Mershon International Studies Review* 38 (1994): 183–207.

Hart, Robert A., Jr., and William Reed. "Selection Effects and Dispute Escalation: Democracy and Status Quo Evaluations." *International Interactions* 25, no. 3 (1999): 243–63.

Henderson, Errol Anthony. "The Democratic Peace Through the Lens of Culture, 1820–1989." *International Studies Quarterly* 42, no. 3 (September 1998): 461–84.

Hermann, Margaret G., and Charles W. Kegley Jr. "Rethinking Democracy and International Peace: Perspectives from Political Psychology." *International Studies Quarterly* 39 (1995): 511–33.

Hewitt, J. Joseph, and Jonathan Wilkenfeld. "Democracies in International Crisis." *International Interactions* 22, no. 2 (1996): 123–42.

James, Patrick, and Glenn E. Mitchell II. "Targets of Covert Pressure: The Hidden Victims of the Democratic Peace." *International Interactions* 21, no. 1 (1995): 85–107.

Kacowicz, Arie M. "Explaining Zones of Peace: Democracies as Satisfied Powers?" *Journal of Peace Research* 32, no. 3 (1995): 265–76.

Kegley, Charles W., Jr., and Margaret Hermann. "How Democracies Use Intervention: A Neglected Dimension in the Studies of the Democratic Peace." *Journal of Peace Research* 33, no. 3 (August 1996): 309–22.

————, and Margaret Hermann. "Military Intervention and the Democratic Peace." *International Interactions* 21, no. 1 (1995): 1–21.

————, and Margaret Hermann. "Putting Military Intervention into the Democratic Peace." *Comparative Political Studies* 30 (1997): 78–107.

Kilgour, D. Marc. "Domestic Political Structure and War Behavior: A Game-Theoretic Approach." *Journal of Conflict Resolution* 35 (June 1991): 266–84.

Kirisci, Kemal. 2002. "The 'Enduring Rivalry' Between Greece and Turkey: Can 'Democratic Peace' Break It?" *Alternatives: Turkish Journal of International Relations* 1, no. 1 (Spring 2002).

Krain, Matthew, and Marissa Edson Myers. "Democracy and Civil War: A Note on the Democratic Peace Proposition." *International Interactions* 23, no. 1 (1997): 109–18.

Lake, David A. "Powerful Pacifists: Democratic States and War." *American Political Science Review* 86 (March 1992): 24–37.

Layne, Christopher. "Kant or Cant: The Myth of the Democratic Peace." *International Security* 19, no. 2 (1992): 5–49.

Levy, Gilat, and Ronny Razin. "It Takes Two: An Explanation for the Democratic Peace." *Journal of the European Economic Association* 2, no. 1 (March 2004): 1–29.

Levy, Jack S. "The Causes of War and the Conditions of Peace." *Annual Review of Political Science* 1 (1998): 139–66.

————. "The Democratic Peace Hypothesis: From Description to Explanation." *Mershon International Studies Review* 38 (October 1994): 352–54.

Mansfield, Edward D. "Democratization and War." *Foreign Affairs* 74 (May–June 1995): 79–97.

————, and Jack Snyder. "Democratization and the Danger of War." *International Security* 20, no. 1 (1995): 5–38.

————, and Jack Snyder. "Democratization and War." *Foreign Affairs* 74, no. 3 (May–June 1995): 79–97.

————, and Jack Snyder. "The Effects of Democratization on War." *International Security* 20, no. 4 (Spring 1996): 196–207.

————, and Jack Snyder. "A Reply to Thompson and Tucker." *Journal of Conflict Resolution* 41, no. 3 (June 1997): 457–61.

Maoz, Zeev. "The Controversy over the Democratic Peace: Rearguard Action, or Cracks in the Wall?" *International Security* 22, no. 1 (Summer 19979): 162–98.

————. "Normative and Structural Causes of Democratic Peace, 1946–1986." *American Political Science Review* 87 (September 1993): 624–38.

————. "Realist and Cultural Critiques of the Democratic Peace: A Theoretical and Empirical Re-Assessment." *International Interactions* 24, no. 1 (1998): 3–89.

————, and Bruce Russett. "Alliance, Contiguity, Distance, Wealth, and Political Stability: Is the Lack of Conflict Among Democracies a Statistical Artifact?" *International Interactions* 17 no. 3 (1992): 245–68.

————, and Bruce Russett. "Normative and Structural Causes of the Democratic Peace, 1946–1986." *American Political Science Review* 87, no. 3 (September 1993): 624–38.

————, and Nasrin Abdolali. "Regime Type and International Conflict, 1817–1976." *Journal of Conflict Resolution* 33, no. 1 (March 1989): 3–35.

Merritt, Richard L., and Dina A. Zinnes. "Democracies and War." In *On Measuring Democracy: Its Consequences and Concomitants,* edited by Alex Inkeles, 207–34. New Brunswick, NJ: Transaction Publishers, 1991.

Mesauita, Bruce Bueno De, and Randolph Siverson. "War and the Survival of Political Leaders: A Comparative Study of Regime Types and Political Accountability." *American Political Science Review* 89, no. 4 (December 1995): 841–56.

Mintz, Alex, and Nehemia Geva. "Why Don't Democracies Fight Each Other? An Experimental Study." *Journal of Conflict Resolution* 37, no. 3 (1993): 484–503.

Modelski, G., and Gardner Perry III. "Democratization in Long Perspective." *Technological Forecasting and Social Change* 39, nos. 1–2 (March–April 1991): 22–34.

Morgan, T. Clifton, and Sally Howard Campbell. "Domestic Structure, Decisional Constraints, and War—So Why Kant Democracies Fight?" *Journal of Conflict Resolution* 35, no. 2 (June 1991): 187–211.

———, and Valerie L. Schwebach. "Take Two Democracies and Call Me in the Morning: A Prescription for Peace?" *International Interactions* 17 (1992): 305–20.

Mousseau, Michael. "Democracy and Compromise in Militarized Interstate Conflicts, 1816–1992." *Journal of Conflict Resolution* 42, no. 2 (April 1998): 210–30.

———. "Democracy and Militarized Interstate Collaboration." *Journal of Peace Research* 34, no. 1 (February 1997): 73–87.

———. "The Nexus of Market Society, Liberal Preferences, and Democratic Peace: Interdisciplinary Theory and Evidence." *International Studies Quarterly* 47 (2003): 483–510.

Oneal, John, and Bruce Russett. "Assessing the Liberal Peace with Alternative Specifications: Trade Reduces Conflict." *Journal of Peace Research* 36 no. 4 (1999): 423–32.

———, and Bruce Russett. "The Classical Liberals Were Right: Democracy, Interdependence, and Conflict, 1950–1985." *International Studies Quarterly* 41, no. 2 (June 1997): 267–94.

———, and Bruce Russett. "Is the Liberal Peace Just an Artifact of Cold War Interests? Assessing Recent Critiques." *International Interactions* 25, no. 3 (1999): 213–41.

———, and Bruce Russett. "The Kantian Peace: The Pacific Benefits of Democracy, Interdependence, and International Organizations, 1885–1992." *World Politics* 52, no. 1 (1999): 1–37.

———, and Bruce Russett. "Why 'An Identified Systemic Analysis of the Democracy-Peace Nexus' Does Not Persuade." *Peace and Defense Economics* 11, no. 2 (2000): 197–214.

————, Frances H. Oneal, Zeev Maoz, and Bruce Russett. "The Liberal Peace: Interdependence, Democracy, and International Conflict, 1950–1985." *Journal of Peace Research* 33, no. 1 (February 1996): 11–28.

Oren, Ido. "The Subjectivity of the 'Democratic' Peace: Changing U.S. Perceptions of Imperial Germany." *International Security* 20, no. 2 (Fall 1995): 147–85.

Owen, John. "How Liberalism Produces Democratic Peace." *International Security* 19, no. 2 (Fall 1994): 87–125.

Ozkececi-Taner, Binnur. "The Myth of Democratic Peace: Theoretical and Empirical Shortcomings of the 'Democratic Peace Theory.'" *Alternatives: Turkish Journal of International Relations* 1, no. 3 (2002).

Peceny, Mark. "A Constructivist Interpretation of the Liberal Peace: The Ambiguous Case of the Spanish-American War." *Journal of Peace Research* 34, no. 4 (November 1997): 415–30.

Peterson, Susan. "How Democracies Differ: Public Opinion, State Structure, and the Lessons from the Fashoda Crisis." *Security Studies* 5, no. 1 (Autumn 1995): 3–37.

Raknerud, Arvid, and Håvard Hegre. "The Hazard of War: Reassessing the Evidence for the Democratic Peace." *Journal of Peace Research* 34, no. 4 (November 1997): 385–404.

Ray, James Lee. "Anarchy Versus Democracy in Post-Cold War Europe." In *Democratic Peace for Europe: Myth or Reality?* edited by Gustaaf Geeraerts and Patrick Stouthuysen. Brussels, Belgium: Free University of Brussels Press, 1999.

————. "The Abolition of Slavery and the End of International War." *International Organization* 43 (1989): 405–39.

————. "The Answer, or an Answer? Evaluating the Democratic Peace Proposition." *Mershon International Studies Review* 42, supp. 2 (November 1998): 369–71.

————. "Democracy and Peace: Then and Now." *International Historical Review* 23 (December 2001): 784–98.

———. "The Democratic Path to Peace." *Journal of Democracy* 8, no. 2 (April 1997): 49–64.

———. "Does Democracy Cause Peace?" In *Annual Review of Political Science,* edited by Nelson W. Polsby, 27–46. Palo Alto, CA: Annual Reviews, 1998.

———. "Does Interstate War Have a Future?" *Conflict Management and Peace Science* 19 (Spring 2002): 53–80.

———. "Integrating Levels of Analysis in World Politics." *Journal of Theoretical Politics* 13 (October 2001): 355–88.

———. "Lakatosian View of the Democratic Peace Research Program: Does It Falsify Realism (or Neorealism)?" In *Progress in International Relations Theory: Metrics and Methods of Scientific Change,* edited by Miriam Fendius Elman and Colin Elman. Boston: MIT Press, 2003.

———. "On the Level(s): Does Democracy Correlate with Peace?" In *What Do We Know About War?* edited by John A. Vasquez. Lanham, MD: Rowman and Littlefield, 2000.

———. "R. J. Rummel's *Understanding Conflict and War:* An Overlooked Classic?" *Conflict Management and Peace Science* 16, no. 2 (1998): 27–49.

———. "Reflections on Millenniums, Old and New: Toward Better Theories About Global Politics." In *Millennial Reflections on International Studies,* edited by Michael Brecher and Frank Harvey. Ann Arbor: University of Michigan Press, 2002.

———. "Wars Between Democracies: Rare, or Nonexistent." *International Interactions* 18, no. 3 (1993): 251–76.

———, with Brandon Valeriano. "Barriers to Replication in Systematic Empirical Research on World Politics." *International Studies Perspectives* 4 (February 2003): 79–85.

———, with Bruce Bueno De Mesquita. "The National Interest Versus Individual Political Ambition: Democracy, Autocracy, and the Reciprocation of Force and Violence in Militarized Interstate Disputes." In *Toward a Scientific Understanding of War,* edited by Paul Diehl. Ann Arbor: University of Michigan Press, 2004.

Raymond, Gregory. "Democracies, Disputes, and Third-Party Intermediaries." *Journal of Conflict Resolution* 38, no. 1 (March 1994): 24–42.

Reiter, Dan, and Allan C. Stam III. "Democracy, War Initiation, and Victory." *American Political Science Review* 92, no. 2 (June 1998): 377–89.

Remmer, Karen L. "Does Democracy Promote Interstate Cooperation? Lessons from the Mercosur Region." *International Studies Quarterly* 42, no. 1 (March 1998): 25–51.

Risse-Kappen, Thomas. "Democratic Peace–Warlike Democracies? A Social Constructivist Interpretation of the Liberal Argument." *European Journal of International Relations* 1, no. 4 (December 1995): 491–518.

Rittberger, Volker. "On the Peace Capacity of Democracies: Reflections on the Political Theory of Peace." *Law and State* 39 (1989): 40–57.

Rothstein, Robert L. "Democracy, Conflict, and Development in the Third World." *Washington Quarterly* 14 (Spring 1991): 46–63.

Rousseau, David L., Christopher Gelpi, Dan Reiter, and Paul Huth. "Assessing the Dyadic Nature of the Democratic Peace." *American Political Science Review* 90, no. 3 (September 1996): 512–33.

Roy, Denny. "Neorealism and Kant: No Pacific Union." *Journal of Peace Research* 30 no. 4 (1993): 451–54.

Rummel, R. J. "A Catastrophe Theory Model of the Conflict Helix with Tests." *Behavioral Science* 32 (October 1987): 241–66.

———. "Democracies Are Less Warlike than Other Regimes." *European Journal of International Relations* 1, no. 4 (December 1995): 457–79.

———. "Democracy, Power, Genocide, and Mass Murder." *Journal of Conflict Resolution* 39, no. 1 (March 1995): 3–26.

———. "Freedom of the Press: A Way to Peace." *ASNE Bulletin* (February 1989): 27.

———. "Libertarian Propositions on Violence Within and Between Nations: A Test Against Published Research Results," *Journal of Conflict Resolution* 29 (September 1985): 419–55.

———. "Libertarianism, Violence Within States, and the Polarity Principle." *Comparative Politics* 16 (July 1984): 443–62.

———. "Political Systems, Violence, and War." In *Approaches to Peace: An Intellectual Map,* edited by W. Scott Thompson et al. Washington, DC: U.S. Institute of Peace, 1992.

———. "Waging Peace Through Democracy." *Waging Peace Bulletin* 4 (Winter 1994–95).

Russett, Bruce. "And Yet It Moves" (Correspondence on the Democratic Peace). *International Security* 19, no. 4 (Spring 1995): 164–75.

———. "Can a Democratic Peace Be Built?" *International Interactions* 18 no. 3 (1993): 277–82.

———. "Counterfactuals About War and Its Absence." In *Counterfactual Thought Experiments in World Politics: Logical, Methodological, and Psychological Perspectives,* edited by Philip E. Tetlock and Aaron Belkin, 171–86. Princeton, NJ: Princeton University Press, 1996.

———. "The Democratic Peace: 'And Yet It Moves.'" *International Security* 19, no. 4 (Spring 1995): 164–77.

———. "From Containment to Democratic Peace." *World Politics* 47, no. 2 (January 1995): 268–82.

———. "A More Democratic and Therefore More Peaceful World." *World Futures* 29, no. 4 (1990): 243–63.

———. "A Neo-Kantian Perspective: Democracy, Interdependence, and International Organizations." In *Security Communities in Comparative and Historical Perspective,* edited by Emanuel Adler and Michael Barnett. Cambridge, UK: Cambridge University Press, 1998.

———. "Peace Among Democracies." *Scientific American* (November 1993): 120.

———. "Peace and the Moral Imperative of Democracy." In *Peacemaking: Moral and Policy Challenges for a New World,* edited by Gerard F. Powers et al. Washington, DC: U.S. Catholic Conference, 1994

———. "Toward a More Democratic and Therefore More Peaceful World." In *Alternative Security: Living Without Nuclear Deterrence,* edited by Burns Weston. Boulder, CO: Westview, 1990.

———, and Harvey Starr. "From Democratic Peace to Kantian Peace: Democracy and Conflict in the International System." In *Handbook of War Studies II,* edited by Manus I. Midlarsky. Ann Arbor: University of Michigan Press, 2000.

———, and James Lee Ray. "Why the Democratic Peace Proposition Lives." [Response to Cohen 1994]. *Review of International Studies* 21, no. 3 (July 1995): 319–23.

———, John Oneal, and David R. Davis. "The Third Leg of the Kantian Tripod For Peace: International Organizations and Militarized Disputes, 1950–1985." *International Organization* 52, no. 3 (Summer 1998): 441–67.

———, John R. Oneal, and Michaelene Cox. "Clash of Civilizations, or Realism and Liberalism Déjà Vu? Some Evidence." *Journal of Peace Research* 37, no. 5 (September 2000): 583–608.

———, and William Antholis. "Do Democracies Rarely Fight Each Other? Evidence from the Peloponnesian War." *Journal of Peace Research* 29 (1992): 415–34.

Schweller, Randall. "Domestic Structure and Preventative War: Are Democracies More Pacific?" *World Politics* 44 (January 1992): 235–69.

Senese, Paul. "Between Dispute and War: The Effect of Joint Democracy on Interstate Conflict Escalation." *Journal of Politics* 59, no. 1 (February 1979): 1–27.

Sherman, Martin. "What Brings Peace, Wealth or Democracy?" *Middle East Quarterly* 5, no. 3 (September 1998): 13–22.

Siverson, Randolph M. "Democracies and War Participation: In Defense of the Institutional Constraints Argument." *European Journal of International Relations* 1, no. 4 (December 1995): 481–90.

———, and Juliann Emmons. "Birds of a Feather: Democratic Political Systems and Alliances Choices in the Twentieth Century." *Journal of Conflict Resolution* 35 (1991): 285–306.

Small, Melvin, and J. David Singer. "The War Proneness of Democratic Regimes, 1816–1965." *Jerusalem Journal of International Relations* 1, no. 4 (Summer 1976): 50–69.

Spiro, David E. "The Insignificance of the Liberal Peace." *International Security* 19, no. 2 (Fall 1994): 50–86.

———. "And Yet It Squirms." *International Security* 19 (Spring 1995): 177–80.

Starr, Harvey. "Democracy and Integration: Why Democracies Don't Fight Each Other." *Journal of Peace Research* 34, no. 2 (May 1997): 153–62.

———. "Democracy and War: Choice, Learning and Security Communities." *Journal of Peace Research* 29, no. 2 (1992): 207–13.

———. "Why Don't Democracies Fight One Another? Evaluating the Theory-Findings Feedback Loop." *Jerusalem Journal of International Relations* 14 no. 4 (1992): 41–59.

Teusch, Ulrich, and Martin Kahl. "Ein Theorem mit Verfallsdatum? Der 'Demokratische Frieden' im Kontext der Globalisierung." In *Zeitschrift für Internationale Beziehungen* 8, no. 2 (2001): 287–320.

Thompson, W. R., and R. Tucker. "A Tale of Two Democratic Peace Critiques." *Journal of Conflict Resolution* 41, no. 3 (1997): 428–54.

Thompson, William. "Democracy and Peace: Putting the Cart Before the Horse?" *International Organization* 50, no. 1 (1996): 141–74.

Van Belle, Douglas A. "Press Freedom and the Democratic Peace." *Journal of Peace Research* 34, no. 4 (November 1997): 405–14.

Väyrynen, Raimo. "Bipolarity, Multipolarity, and Domestic Political Systems." *Journal of Peace Research* 32, no. 3 (1995): 361–71.

Vincent, Jack. "Freedom and International Conflict: Another Look" and "On Rummel's Omnipresent Theory." *International Studies Quarterly* 31, no. 1 (March 1987): 103–12, 119–26.

———. "The Relative Importance of Power, Economic Development, and Political System During the Middle of the Cold War." *Journal of Peace Research* 2 (1996).

Wagner, Wolfgang. "Building an Internal Security Community: The Democratic Peace and the Politics of Extradition in Western Europe." *Journal of Peace Research* 40, no. 6 (2003): 695–712.

Walt, Stephen M. "Never Say Never: Wishful Thinking on Democracy and War." *Foreign Affairs* 78, no. 1 (1999): 146–51.

Ward, Michael D., and Kristian S. Gleditsch. "Democratizing for Peace." *American Political Science Review* 92, no. 1 (March 1998): 51–61.

Weart, Spencer R. "Peace Among Democratic and Oligarchic Republics." *Journal of Peace Research* 31 no. 3 (1994): 299–316.

———. "Why They Don't Fight: Democracies, Oligarchies, and Peace." *In Brief,* no. 48. Washington, DC: U.S. Institute of Peace, 1993.

Weede, Erich. "Democracy and War Involvement." *Journal of Conflict Resolution* 28 (1984): 649–64.

———. "Economic Policy and International Security: Rent-Seeking, Free Trade and Democratic Peace." *European Journal of International Relations* 1, no. 4 (December 1995): 519–38.

———. "Some New Evidence on Correlates of Political Violence: Income Inequality, Regime Repressiveness, and Economic Development." *European Sociological Review* 3 (1987): 97–108.

———. "Some Simple Calculations on Democracy and War Involvement." *Journal of Peace Research* 29, no. 4 (1992): 377–83.

Wildavsky, Aaron. "No War Without Dictatorship, No Peace Without Democracy: Foreign Policy as Domestic Politics." *Social Philosophy and Policy* 3, no. 1 (Autumn 1985): 176–91.

Wolf, Klaus Dieter. "Capitalism and War: Globalism Meets the Democratic Peace." *Mershon International Studies Review* 39 (1995): 239–45.

BOOKS

Aklaev, Airat R. *Democratization and Ethnic Peace: Patterns of Ethnopolitical Crisis Management in Post-Soviet Settings.* Aldershot: Ashgate, 1999.

Barkawi, Tarak, and Mark Laffey, eds. *Democracy, Liberalism, and War: Rethinking the Democratic Peace Debate.* Transformations in Politics and Society. Boulder, CO: Rienner. 2001

Bohman, James, and Matthias Lutz-Bachmann, eds. *Perpetual Peace: Essays on Kant's Cosmopolitan Ideal.* Cambridge, MA: MIT Press, 1997.

Brown, Michael E., and Steven E. Miller. *Debating the Democratic Peace.* Cambridge, MA: MIT Press, 1996.

Elman, Miriam Fendius, ed. *Paths to Peace: Is Democracy the Answer?* Cambridge, MA: MIT Press, 1997.

Forsyth, James W., Jr. "Through the Glass Darkly: An Examination of Liberal and Repressive Regimes and War, 1945–1988." PhD diss., University of Denver, 1999.

Geeraerts, G., Patrick Stouthuysen, and Gustaaf Geeraerts, eds. *Democratic Peace for Europe: Myth or Reality?* Brussels, Belgium: VUB University Press, 1999.

Gilbert, Alan. *Must Global Politics Constrain Democracy? Great-Power Realism, Democratic Peace, and Democratic Internationalism.* Princeton, NJ: Princeton University Press, 1999.

Gleditsch, Kristian Skrede. *All International Politics Is Local: The Diffusion of Conflict, Integration, and Democratization.* Ann Arbor: University of Michigan Press, 2002.

Gowa, Joanne. *Ballots and Bullets: The Elusive Democratic Peace.* Princeton, NJ: Princeton University Press, 2000.

Howard, Michael. *War and the Liberal Conscience.* New Brunswick, NJ: Rutgers University Press, 1978.

Huth, Paul K., and Todd L. Allee. *The Democratic Peace and Territorial Conflict in the Twentieth Century.* Cambridge, UK: Cambridge University Press, 2002.

Kant, Immanuel. *Perpetual Peace.* Translated by Lewis White Beck. New York: Liberal Arts Press, 1957.

Knüpling, Felix. *Democracies and War: An Investigation of Theoretical Explanations.* New Brunswick, NJ: Transaction Publishers, 2001.

Leatherman, Janie. *From Cold War to Democratic Peace: Third Parties, Peaceful Change, and the OSCE.* Syracuse, NY: Syracuse University Press, 2003.

Lipson, Charles. *Reliable Partners: How Democracies Have Made a Separate Peace.* Princeton, NJ: Princeton University Press, 2003.

Macmillan, John. *On Liberal Peace: Democracy, War and the International Order.* New York: Tauris, 1998.

Moore, John Norton. *Solving the War Puzzle: Beyond the Democratic Peace.* Durham, NC: Carolina Academic Press, 2004.

Owen, John M., IV. *Liberal Peace, Liberal War: American Politics and International Security.* Ithaca, NY: Cornell University Press, 1997.

———. "Testing the Democratic Peace: American Diplomatic Crises, 1794–1917." PhD diss., Harvard University, 1993.

Rasler, Karen, and William R. Thompson. *Puzzles of the Democratic Peace: Theory, Geopolitics and the Transformation of World Politics.* Evolutionary Processes in World Politics. New York: Palgrave Macmillan, 2005.

Ray, James Lee. *Democracy and International Conflict: An Evaluation of the Democratic Peace Proposition.* Columbia: University of South Carolina Press, 1995.

Reychler, Luc. *Democratic Peace-Building and Conflict Prevention: The Devil Is in the Transition.* Leuven, Belgium: Leuven University Press, 1999.

Rousse, Stéphane. *The North American Democratic Peace: Absence of War and Security Institution-Building in Canadians-U.S. Relations, 1867–1958.* Montreal: McGill-Queen's University Press, 2004.

Rummel, R. J. *Death by Government.* New Brunswick, NJ: Transaction Publishers, 1994.

———. *The Miracle That Is Freedom: The Solution to War, Violence, Genocide, and Poverty.* Martin Monograph Series, no. 1. Moscow, ID: University of Idaho Press, 1996.

———. *Never Again: Ending War, Democide, and Famine Through Democratic Freedom.* Coral Springs, FL: Llumina Publications, 2005.

———. *Power Kills: Democracy as a Method of Nonviolence.* New Brunswick, NJ: Transaction Publishers, 1997.

———. "Saving Lives, Enriching Life: Freedom as a Right and a Moral Good." www.hawaii.edu/powerkills/note15.htm.

———. *Statistics of Democide: Genocide and Mass Murder Since 1900.* Münster, Germany: Lit Verlag; Piscatway, NJ: Transaction Publishers, 1998.

———. *Understanding Conflict and War,* Vol. 4, *War, Power, Peace.* Beverly Hills, CA: Sage Publications, 1997.

———. *Understanding Conflict and War,* Vol. 5, *The Just Peace.* Beverly Hills, CA: Sage Publications, 1981.

Russett, Bruce. *Grasping the Democratic Peace: Principles for a Post-Cold War World.* Princeton, NJ: Princeton University Press, 2001.

———, and John Oneal. *Triangulating Peace: Democracy, Interdependence, and International Organizations.* New York: Norton, 2001.

Singer, Max, and Aaron Wildavsky. *The Real World Order: Zones of Peace/Zones of Turmoil.* Chatham, NJ: Chatham House, 1993.

Snyder, Jack. *From Voting to Violence: Democratization and Nationalist Conflict.* New York: Norton, 2000.

Sondhi, M. L., ed. *Democratic Peace: The Foreign Policy Implications.* New Delhi: Har-Anand, 2000.

Stremlau, John J. *A House No Longer Divided: Progress and Prospects for Democratic Peace in South Africa.* Leuven: Leuven University Press, 1999.

Weart, Stewart. *Never at War: Why Democracies Will Not Fight One Another.* New Haven, CT: Yale University Press, 1998.

INDEX

INDEX

Turkmenistan, 12
Tutsi, 78–80

Ukraine, 86
United Nations, 12, 62, 80
Universal Declaration of Human
  Rights, 18

Vietnam, 45, 81, 85–86

war, 11, 13–16, 23–24, 45–46,
  48–51, 54–55, 63, 67, 70–73,
76, 81, 86, 88, 93, 95, 99–100,
  102–13, 115–17
West Germany, 54
World War I, 107
World War II, 23, 50, 54, 76, 100,
  107, 112

Yagoda, Genrikh, 88
Yezhov, Nikolai, 87, 91
Yugoslavia, 45